# LOUIS ARMSTRONG

1931

Macmillan Publishing Company
New York
Collier Macmillan Publishers
London

1931

# LOUIS
# ARMSTRONG
## AN AMERICAN SUCCESS STORY

### JAMES LINCOLN COLLIER

1935

Macmillan books are available at special discounts for bulk purchases for sales promotions, premiums, fund raising, or educational use. Special editions or book excerpts can also be created to specification. For details, contact:
Special Sales Director
Macmillan Publishing Company
866 Third Avenue
New York, N.Y. 10022

Photographs courtesy of the Frank Driggs collection

Macmillan Publishing Company
866 Third Avenue, New York, N.Y. 10022
Collier Macmillan Canada, Inc.
Printed in the United States of America
10 9 8 7 6 5 4 3

**Library of Congress Cataloging in Publication Data**
Collier, James Lincoln, date.
  Louis Armstrong: An American success story.
  "If you want to know more about Louis Armstrong—":p.
  Summary: A biography of one of America's most important musicians, who was born in extreme poverty and never had a real music lesson, but became world famous for his singing and trumpet playing.
    1. Armstrong, Louis, 1900–1971—Juvenile literature. 2. Jazz musicians—United States—Biography—Juvenile literature. [1. Armstrong, Louis,  1900–1971.   2. Musicians.   3. Afro-Americans—Biography]
I. Title.
ML3930.A75C67  1985      785.42'092'4 [B] [92]      84–42982
ISBN 0-02-722830-4

For Jackie, Cindy and Lisa

1934

# LOUIS ARMSTRONG

1949

He was a little black boy playing in a dusty back-yard of a paint-peeling shack at the end of an alley in a slum in New Orleans at the turn of the century. The shack had no toilet. Water came from a cistern that was filled by rain. He was wearing a dress, the only piece of clothing he owned. His toys were twigs and pebbles and pieces of broken junk he happened to find. His only parent was his grandmother; his father had disowned him at birth and his mother was off some place—where, he did not know. He had never had a birthday party for the simple reason that he did not know when he was born. He had never had a Christmas tree nor, indeed, even a Christmas; that was a holiday for wealthy people who had electricity and running water in the house. He ate mostly beans and rice and fish-head stew and stale bread.

He was at the absolute bottom of American society—there was nobody lower but the dogs, and even many dogs in the United States lived better than he did. He was born in the South at a time when a black boy could expect nothing but to grow up, work hard at the lowest jobs all his life, and hope that he could somehow, somewhere, manage to stay healthy and get a little something out of life for himself.

The little boy playing in the dust, however, was a genius. He would never have a real music lesson in his life, would be too poor to buy a musical instrument of his own until he was seventeen years old, would not learn to read music until he was over twenty, and for the whole of his long career would play so incorrectly that he would ruin his lip. Yet he would change the nature of music in America and much of the rest of the world.

He would never go further than third grade in a poor, segregated slum school where he would learn to read and write a little, add and subtract a little, and not much else. Yet he would go on to play for presidents, kings, and queens, become the subject of a half-dozen biographies, and be revered not only as one of the most famous entertainers of his time, but also as the greatest jazz musician who ever lived.

The story of Louis Armstrong is fascinating, and it could only have happened in America. It is a story that tells us much about the relationships between blacks and whites in America, about the hard, commercial entertainment business, about the soul of America itself. How could this poor, obscure black boy overcome virtually every handicap it was possible to have, to become one of the most important artists of his century?

In order to understand that story, we must understand something about the people and the place Louis came from. That is not easy. Most of the old records are lost. There are no birth certificates for either him or his parents. We know where he went to school, but the school is gone and so are the records, so we do not know what he studied and what kind of grades he got. His mother read and wrote only a little, his father not at all, and they left no bundles of letters filled with little stories about Louis. None of them kept a diary, and they were too poor to gather souvenirs like picture postcards of trips they made, programs from shows they saw, albums of photographs of Louis on his first day at school or blowing his first cornet. They were too poor to go on trips, see shows, buy a camera. About all we have from Louis's youth are two pictures showing an undersized but determined-looking boy.

Fortunately, many people from Louis's neighborhood have told their stories. Louis also wrote of his youth in a book called *Satchmo: My Life in New Orleans*. This is helpful, but not as helpful as it might be, because Louis changed some of the facts around to make a better tale of it. And out of these things we can piece together a pretty fair picture of how Louis grew up.

He was born in the city of New Orleans, probably sometime in 1898. The city stands near the mouth of the Mississippi. It was founded in 1718 by French colonists, who were busy making a huge empire throughout the Caribbean, based on sugar. Growing sugar cane and turning it into sugar was hot, hard, dirty work. To do it the French and other colonists, like the English and Dutch, brought over from Africa hundreds of thousands of black people as slaves. Some of these blacks had been captured by white slave hunters, but most of them were prisoners of war, criminals, or debtors who had been sold into slavery by other black tribesmen. A huge number of these black slaves ended up in the United States, where most of them worked out their lives on plantations in the South. Freed after the Civil War, at first they looked forward to developing themselves, through education, and becoming part of American society. However, white Southerners, bitter at losing the war and angered to find former slaves sitting in Congress and owning businesses, set about pushing the blacks back into slavery. Through beatings, hangings, and burnings, they intimidated blacks and then rammed through laws officially segregating blacks from the white system. By the time of Louis Armstrong's birth, blacks were confined to slums. Virtually all of the southern blacks were forced to spend their lives at menial labor, working in white people's kitchens, on the docks loading ships, in the baking hot fields hoeing corn, cotton, and tobacco.

Things were little better in the North. There ambitious black children could get some kind of an education; a few, if they were lucky, could develop businesses of their own in black communities; and a handful could become lawyers, doctors, teachers. But even in the North around the turn of the century, blacks were segregated from the mainstream of society. Blacks could not go to white theaters, white dances, white restaurants. They had to live in their own neighborhoods, attend their own schools, go to their own nightclubs. Young black athletes could not aspire to join professional athletic teams or play in orchestras or act in movies; these places were reserved for whites. Blacks had to put together their own baseball leagues and dance orchestras.

This, then, is the first thing we have to understand about Louis Armstrong: He was black. He could not wander freely around his own city, outside the black ghetto where he was raised, the way white boys could. There were many places where blacks could not go unless they had definite business there, such as delivering coal or mowing lawns. Louis could not go to shows and movies—blacks were barred from them. He could not go to restaurants except cheap ones meant for blacks; he could not even go into a white family's house through the front door. He had to treat whites, even white children his own age, with respect, and take off his hat to them. When they told him to do something he could not argue, but had to say, "Yassah, boss, yassah," and do it.

The second thing we have to understand about Louis Armstrong is how much he was neglected by his family. His father was named Willie Armstrong. He was a handsome man, Louis said later, and he liked to wear a uniform and march at the head of parades, which are a custom of New Orleans. He worked in a factory running a boiler in which turpentine was distilled—terribly hot, hard work in a southern climate. Eventually he rose to become "straw boss," that is to say, a kind of foreman over the other black workers. (He could not, of course, be a boss of whites.) This was quite a success for an illiterate black man in that period.

However, he rarely paid any attention to his son. By the time Louis was going to school Willie Armstrong had married another woman and was raising another family, and, even though he lived only a few blocks from Louis, he never bothered to come to see him. Sometimes Louis would see him marching down the street in his fancy uniform at the head of a parade, looking handsome and important, and he would wish that somehow he could make his father care for him. But he never could.

Louis's mother was named Mayann. She was short and fat, cheerful, and liked to have a good time. She was born in a little farm town outside New Orleans called Boutte. Times were difficult for farmers and jobs hard to get, so as a teenager Mayann, like a lot of blacks, moved into the city. Jobs were scarce there, too, and Mayann took whatever she could find, which was not much. Sometimes she got work cleaning people's houses or doing laundry.

For the first year of Louis's life he and Mayann lived with Louis's grandmother, Josephine Armstrong, in a little run-down shack with a dusty yard at the end of Jane Alley. That dilapidated neighborhood was so tough it was called the Battlefield. Even as a boy Louis saw knife fights.

Josephine Armstrong made her money washing white people's laundry. Sometimes she would go to their houses to do it. Other times she would bring the laundry home. Louis would sit in the yard, watching his grandmother light a fire in a coal brazier—a kind of simple fireplace, like a small barbecue stove. She would put a big tub of water on the fire and, when it was hot, put in the clothes and scrub them with a coarse bar of yellow soap. Josephine could make fifty cents or a dollar a day doing laundry. It was just barely enough to buy rice and beans and scraps of meat and fish to feed the family.

When Louis was about a year old, his mother left and moved into a small apartment on Perdido Street near the corner of Liberty, about eighteen blocks away from Jane Alley. She came to visit him sometimes, but he missed her. However, his grandmother took good care of him. She was strict and would give him a whipping with a bit of stick from a tree when he misbehaved. On Sundays, she took him to church, where he got his first experience singing.

But they were very poor. They ate the simplest kind of food, many times nothing but beans or rice for dinner several nights in a row. Louis never wore shoes—his grandmother could not afford to buy him a pair. He wore dresses until he was a young boy and, after that, hand-me-down trousers and blue shirts. He never owned more than two or three pieces of clothing at a time. He had no toys or books, and if he had ever appeared with a football or a baseball glove or a bicycle, people would have assumed that he had stolen it and called the police.

When Louis was about seven his mother sent for him to come and live with her in the apartment on Perdido Street. She now had a little daughter named Beatrice, whom the family always called Mama Lucy. Mayann needed Louis to help with the child while she worked. Louis was very happy to join his mother. Even though Mayann had left Louis with his grandmother, Louis knew that his mother really cared for him. He loved her and wanted to live with her.

He was also happy to be moving to Perdido Street because that neighborhood was much more exciting than Jane Alley. The area had been specially marked out as an entertainment district for blacks by the city of New Orleans. It was rough, as tough a place as Louis's old neighborhood, the Battlefield. It was run down, too. Most of the buildings were one or two stories high, made of wood, and usually had the paint peeling from them. The streets were dirt—dusty in the dry weather, muddy the rest of the time. Most of the area was given over to dance halls, houses of prostitution, and saloons, which were called "honky-tonks" or just "tonks." The tonks were very rough bars. There would be a barroom in front, a room for dancing, and a back room for gambling at cards or dice. Every night, and much of the day, too, the tonks were filled with tough working men, mostly black, but some white, who came there because the drinks and the women were cheap. There were fights in the tonks every night. Knives and guns were drawn frequently; people were often wounded and sometimes killed. The tonks were smoky, noisy places where drugs were sold openly.

Louis's neighborhood around Perdido Street was not the only entertainment district in the city. There was another one not far away, reserved for whites. This was the famous Storyville. As in Louis's district, here were saloons, restaurants, gambling joints, and houses of prostitution. The neighborhood was more expensive than the black entertainment district, larger, a little cleaner and fancier, and not quite so tough. Thousands of tourists came to Storyville every year to be entertained and spend their money; it was famous around the United States, and many people thought it was glamorous. But a lot of things that went on in Storyville were not very glamorous when seen close up. There was plenty of alcoholism and drug addiction, and it was filled with teenaged girls, some of them as young as twelve, who were working as prostitutes. Many of them had run away from home, attracted by what they thought was the freedom and glamour of Storyville. Others were enticed, or even forced, into prostitution. Neither entertainment district, black or white (hereafter referred to as black Storyville and white Storyville), was as picturesque as many writers made out.

Louis's life in his new neighborhood was better than his life on Jane Alley, but not much better. He lived in a small three-room apartment on the second floor of a cement-block building, one of the few in the neighborhood not made of wood. There was a balcony running along the second floor, with stairs going down to the ground on the outside of the building. The door to the apartment opened onto the balcony.

Mayann did odd jobs for a living, mostly doing laundry as Josephine did. There was still little money, and they ate the same sort of food—rice, beans, fish stews, scraps of meat—that he had eaten at his grandmother's house.

Mayann was not much interested in church, and did not make Louis go. However, a block away was a little school for black children called the Fisk School. Louis started his schooling here. Because Fisk was for blacks, the city of New Orleans did not lavish money on it. There were not enough books, and the few they had were old, dirty, and torn. There were no globes, encyclopedias, or science displays. The school did not even have a cafeteria. Louis brought his lunch from home. For a while Mayann had a boyfriend who worked as a waiter in a hotel. He would keep the leftovers from the diners' plates, such as partly eaten pieces of chicken or pork chops, and bring them to Mayann, who would make Louis's school lunches from them. The leftovers were delicious to him.

Mayann had many boyfriends. Sometimes one of them would move in with the family for a while. Some of these men were kind to Louis, but many of them were not. Most were tough men from the neighborhood, and they frequently got drunk and punched Mayann around. It scared Louis when this happened, and when he got a little bit older he sometimes tried to help Mayann defend herself.

Mayann loved Louis and Mama Lucy and tried to take care of them as best she could, but she was not very reliable. Sometimes she would go off on a drinking spree with her current boyfriend and forget all about her children. When this happened Louis would have to take care of Mama Lucy and himself. Luckily, Louis had an uncle named Isaac Miles living in the neighborhood. Uncle Ike was a stevedore who labored hard all day long, loading barges on the levee. He had six children, though, unhappily, his wife was dead. He was a kindly man, and when Louis and Mama Lucy were left alone, they would go and stay with Uncle Ike. Uncle Ike was so poor that he could afford only one bed. As many kids would pile into the bed as would fit and the rest would sleep on the floor.

But as tough as the neighborhood was, and as poor as it was in most things, it had one thing in abundance: music. An entertainment district is always filled with music, and in Louis's area it was everywhere. There were bands in the dance halls, bands in the tonks, bands parading around in the streets. Louis could not escape the sound of music. He heard it as he dozed off in his bed at night and he heard it coming out of the tonks when he woke up in the morning, for some of the tonks were open around the clock. He heard it in school during the day when bands marched by outside.

Music was as much a part of his life as the mud in the street and the sky above. It was one of the few wholly good things in his life, and quickly he grew to love it.

# CHAPTER TWO

New Orleans has always been a musical city. The French people who founded the city were more interested in fun than in work, and they were constantly giving parties and dances. They liked the opera and the symphony, too, and by the nineteenth century New Orleans had its own opera houses and symphony orchestras.

It also quickly became a "good time" city. There was a reason for this. It was an important port. Until the railroads were built in the second half of the nineteenth century, the only way people could export goods from the vast fertile frontier land between the Allegheny Mountains and the Mississippi River was via the network of rivers that run through the relatively flat countryside. This network empties into the Mississippi, so everything that came out of that huge area of the country, covering what is now seven states, ended up in New Orleans. Millions of dollars' worth of timber, furs, whiskey, cotton, corn, and wheat came into New Orleans every year. Most of it was then loaded into ships and carried away to be sold in the West Indies, in cities on the Atlantic coast of the United States such as Boston, New York, and Philadelphia, or across the ocean to Europe or even China.

Coming along with these goods were thousands of men—sailors on the ships, Mississippi bargemen, lumberers, farmers, trappers coming into the city to sell their goods. These men were flush from selling their logs, furs, and cotton and were out for liquor, women, drugs, dancing, music. Supplying these items became a big business for New Orleans. By the time Louis Armstrong was born, the city had developed a huge entertainment industry catering to sailors, farmers coming into town to sell their produce, riverboat men, and thousands of tourists who came just for the fun. This huge entertainment industry was focused on the black Storyville and white Storyville, but it was also spread throughout the city, and it demanded an extraordinary amount of music.

We must remember that when Louis was growing up, there was no radio, no television. The record player was a tinny, newfangled invention that only the wealthy could afford. The only kind of mechanical music available came from player pianos that played automatically from rolls inserted in the works. For the most part, music was live, made by people, not machines.

There were bands everywhere. In New Orleans people had bands at picnics, bands in parks, bands at baseball games and horse races. To advertise a dance, a boxing match, a department store sale, the promoters would rent a wagon and put a big sign on the side about what they were advertising. Then they would put a band in the wagon and drive around the city all day, attracting audiences to the sign.

The city had a tradition of social clubs, too, black ones for black people, white ones for white. Many of these clubs were "burying societies." Black people, particularly, felt that it was very important to have a decent funeral for themselves, and to be buried in a proper graveyard, not in a pauper's field. Because they knew they would never be able to save much money, if any, and were likely to be very poor when they were old and could not work—there was no such thing as welfare or social security in those days, they had to make provision, while they could, for a proper burial. So they would join together in clubs, each member contributing a small amount every week, such as twenty-five cents. The club members guaranteed each other decent burials. It was customary at these funerals to have bands, which would parade slowly through the streets behind the hearse, playing hymns there and at the graveside. After the service there would be a wake, or party. The band would play a lively march on the way home from the cemetery and then play for dancing at the wake, where there would be much food and drink. These funeral bands were always in the streets when Louis Armstrong was growing up.

Another place where there was music was Lincoln Park. This was an area two or three blocks in size not far away from Louis's Perdido Street neighborhood. Lincoln Park was meant for blacks. There was a dance hall there, a roller skating rink, places for picnicking, and on Sundays there might be movie shows or a balloon ascent. There were regular band concerts at Lincoln Park. Across the street was Johnson Park, which was a rougher place used mainly for picnics and baseball games, but it also had a band. These parks were so much fun that a lot of whites came out, too. This was part of the unfairness of things: Blacks could not go to white places, but whites could come to black ones.

North of the city was Lake Pontchartrain. Because of New Orleans's subtropical climate, people liked to go out to the lake, where it was cooler, especially in summer. There was, of course, no air conditioning in those days; indeed, there were no electric refrigerators, either, but true iceboxes, which were kept cool with blocks of ice.

Because so many New Orleanians came out to the lake to get cool, many restaurants, gambling clubs, and dance pavilions were built there, usually on piers stretched out into the lake where they could catch the breeze. Most of these places were for whites, but at the west end of the resort area there were places for blacks, too. The resorts always had music. Then, too, groups of people would come out to the lake for picnics—sometimes whole social clubs would come—and they would hire bands to come with them.

For black people music was very important. Books were expensive, and many people could not read anyway. They could not get into white theaters to see vaudeville shows or that new invention, the moving picture. Sometimes tent shows for blacks would come to the city, but that was not often. The only kinds of entertainment these blacks had were dancing, gambling, and music. For them music was a vital part of life. It provided one of the few good emotional experiences they could have.

The music that Louis Armstrong heard as he was growing up was extremely diverse. At Lincoln Park the fancy John Robichaux Orchestra played waltzes, quadrilles, and concert pieces taken from operas, as well as popular songs. Louis could not often afford the admission to Lincoln Park, but he could stand outside and hear the band quite well.

At Johnson Park the music was more likely to be rough ragtime played by small bands of five or six pieces. Ragtime was a bouncy, lilting music invented by blacks in the nineteenth century out of a combination of the music they had brought from Africa and the music they found in the United States. Originally, it had probably been played on banjos, but it had developed into a music for the piano. In the early part of this century it was very popular all over the country, with whites as well as blacks, and had been adapted for bands and many combinations of instruments. All bands played a certain amount of ragtime, and some of the black bands Louis heard at Johnson Park and elsewhere specialized in it.

Another source of music was the riverboats. They were basically floating dance halls, and although Louis couldn't afford to go on one, he could hear the bands playing on deck as boats loaded up with passengers and drew away from the dock.

The music that Louis was hearing from the tonks in his own neighborhood was mostly the blues. The blues was another black invention, created around the turn of the century, another combination of African and American music. It was a slow music, with a lot of twisted and bent notes, some of which were not on the ordinary scale and could not be played on the piano. The blues bands in the tonks were very rough. The musicians could not read music, but improvised. Sometimes there would be just guitar and bass fiddle, or guitar and piano. Other times there would be a horn (especially a cornet), clarinet, or trombone, accompanied by a piano and snare drum. The hustlers and their women who hung around the tonks liked to dance the slow drag to the blues.

They also played the blues for slow-drag dancing in the dance halls. One of the most famous of these was called Funky Butt Hall. It was right in Louis's block, a ramshackle building losing its paint. Here, on weekends, there would be dances. Usually the band would play outside for a half hour before the dance to attract a crowd. The crowd that came to these dances was so tough that there was fighting at nearly every dance. The band was placed on a balcony some ten feet above the dance floor so that the musicians would not be hurt when knives flashed and bottles flew. The legendary Buddy Bolden and his band played at Funky Butt Hall. All the time Louis was growing up he heard the bands at Funky Butt Hall. He would stand out front and

listen while the band serenaded the crowd, and then
he would go around to the side to listen through a
crack in the wall and watch the dancers do the slow
drag. The bands at Funky Butt Hall also played
ragtime.

At seven and eight and nine and ten years of age
Louis Armstrong was absorbing an enormous amount
of music. He admired the parade bands with their
bright uniforms, the ragtime bands with their brassy
instruments flashing in the night lights, the solemn-
faced Robichaux men in their formal suits behind their
curved music stands. The sight and sound of it all
seemed wonderful to Louis. He could not imagine that
anything could be finer than to be a musician.

But how was he to manage that? He had no money
to buy an instrument or pay for lessons if he had one.
Even a secondhand cornet in a hock shop would cost
about ten dollars, he knew. Ten dollars was an impossible amount, an amount that would take the family
weeks to save; and there was no hope of the family's
saving any money, Louis knew, because Mayann was
careless and would spend it for drinks, or one of her
boyfriends would take it. All the money Louis ever
had were pennies, nickels, and dimes. And always they
had to go for food for the family. You could buy enough
rice for the family's dinner for a nickel. No, to buy an
instrument was impossible.

Besides, he was shy. It was something he tried to
overcome. There was a pretty girl in his school called
Whilhelmia. She was one of the daughters of Mrs.

Martin, who was head of the school. Louis liked her a lot. But he was too bashful to speak to her and far too bashful to ask her to be his girlfriend.

Being shy made things even harder for him—harder for him to ask people for favors, to push himself forward. If he had had a real father it might have been different. Then he could have said, "Dad, please, I want a cornet," and even though his father was poor, he might have found a way. But there was no hope in that, either.

Yet Louis hoped. Someday, he thought, it would happen. Someday he would find a way to get an instrument and play the music that surrounded him.

# CHAPTER THREE

**E**ven as a small boy Louis was aware that he would have to take on a lot of responsibility for the family. Nobody ever told him so; he just realized that his father would never help, Mayann would let him down at times, and it would be up to him to take care of things. When he was around eight he met an older white boy named Charles, who sold newspapers. Louis managed to make an arrangement with Charles whereby he would supply Louis with papers to sell in his own neighborhood in exchange for part of the profits. Louis could only make pennies from his newspaper route, but even pennies were a help in buying food.

At about the same time Louis discovered a second way of making money. It was not only parade bands that played music in the streets of New Orleans; there were many other kinds of musicians wandering around, too, playing on the levees, the docks, the sidewalks—anywhere they could collect a crowd and earn a few pennies and nickels. Given his love of music, it is not surprising that it would occur to Louis that he might sing in the streets, too. He joined a group of other boys to form a quartet. They rehearsed together, and then they began going through the streets singing.

Mostly they sang old favorites, like "Home, Sweet Home," and popular tunes of the time, such as "My Brazilian Beauty." They sang in four-part harmony. For Louis, singing in the quartet was important because he loved music, and because it brought in a few pennies to help with the household expenses. But the experience of singing in the quartet was most valuable because of the training it gave to his ear. An improvising musician has to be able to hear harmonies in his head as the tune goes along, just the way most of us can see pictures in our heads of places we remember. It takes training to develop this ability to hear harmonies quickly, and although Louis clearly had a great natural gift even as a small boy, he needed to develop it. Louis sang in the streets several times a week for several years. It amounted to a very long course in ear training.

The boys in Louis's quartet all had nicknames. There were Happy Bolton, Big Nose Sidney, and Little Mack. In the New Orleans of that day, if a boy didn't have a nickname he felt left out. Around the neighborhood the people called Louis "Little Louis" because he was short and skinny, but he wanted a better nickname than that. Finally he got one. He was known for his big, broad smile, so the boys began to call him "Dippermouth" because his smile made his mouth look as big as a dipper.

Louis earned some money from singing and from delivering papers, but as he got closer to his teen years, he found other, less respectable ways of making money. One was by playing dice. Crapshooting was very popular among the tough hustlers and sports of the Perdido Street neighborhood, and Louis took up the game. Sometimes he won and sometimes he lost, but when he won he was proud to bring his winnings home to Mayann to help with the family.

He was also, at this time, beginning to steal. He did not steal a lot, for there was not a lot for him to steal in his poor neighborhood, but there were always drunken people around who were careless with their money. Some of the tonks also doubled as small grocery stores, and it was not hard to slip in and steal a banana or two, or some candy from the counter. The truth was, by the time Louis got to be twelve and thirteen, he was a street kid, getting into the kind of trouble that street kids sometimes get into. His heroes, naturally, were the musicians he was hearing at Funky Butt Hall, at the tonks, in the street parades, like Buddie Petit, Bunk Johnson, and others. But there was also another sort of man around the neighborhood whom he admired. They were the hustlers who made their livings by gambling, by keeping prostitutes, by mugging and robbing. These men wore fancy Stetson hats, box-backed coats, tight-fitting pants that they kept well pressed, and high shoes with a glossy shine. Some of them even put little light bulbs in the toes of their shoes, attached by cords that ran up their pants legs to batteries in their pockets. When they wanted to attract the attention of women, they would flash the little lights off and on.

When they were flush with money they spent it lavishly, buying diamonds for their girlfriends, drinks for their friends, fancy clothes for themselves. When they were out of money they stole. These hustlers were the big men of the neighborhood, and Louis looked up to them. One day, he thought, he would be a hustler, too.

He might have become one, but one New Year's Eve something happened to change all that—something crucial to the development of Louis Armstrong as a musician and, thus, to the music of our time.

In New Orleans it was customary to celebrate New Year's Eve with fireworks. Also, sometimes people would shoot off blank cartridges from pistols. On New Year's Eve of 1912 or 1913, Louis went out into the street with the quartet to catch the excitement and make some money by singing for the people out celebrating. Before he left he stuck in his pocket a small pistol loaded with blanks that had been lying around the apartment. It belonged to Mayann's current boyfriend.

He met his friends, and they started off toward the white Storyville district, where they thought business might be good. As they were going along, they ran into another boy, who suddenly began firing blanks at them from a pistol of his own. Instantly Louis pulled out his pistol to shoot back. Almost at the same moment he felt a strong hand on his collar. He looked up. Gripping him tightly was Long John Gorman, a policeman famous in the Perdido Street neighborhood.

Suddenly frightened, Louis stuck the pistol in his pocket and began to blabber out some explanation to Gorman. But Gorman didn't listen. Instead, he took Louis down the street and into the neighborhood police station, where he was locked up for the night. He spent the night there, and the next day, which was New Year's Day, and that night, too, in jail, lonely and scared to death of what might happen to him. On January second Gorman took him into court and told the judge about Louis: He was a street boy who was getting into trouble. Wouldn't it be better to put him somewhere he might straighten himself out? The judge agreed, and he sentenced Louis to a place called The Colored Waifs' Home—indefinitely.

The Colored Waifs' Home had been started by a black man named Joseph Jones, a former soldier, to take care of homeless black boys and other boys who, like Louis, were headed for trouble. It was housed in a collection of ramshackle buildings outside town, near a railroad track. There was a main building two stories high, which had a big dormitory room upstairs where the boys slept, and a mess hall, chapel, and schoolroom downstairs. There were also barns where a couple of cows were kept for milk. There was a garden where vegetables were grown for the use of the home, a parade ground for baseball and for drilling, and beyond the grounds, open fields. The school had little money, and the food was very simple; sometimes the boys would eat only beans and molasses for supper.

The school was run along military lines. Bugle calls

got the boys up in the morning, told them when it was time to eat, and sent them to bed at night. They went through military drill using wooden rifles and wood drums. They also did routine chores: cleaning out the cow barns, hoeing vegetables in the garden, scrubbing floors, and washing up the dishes, pots, and pans in the kitchen after meals.

Louis arrived at the Waifs' Home scared and heartsick. He had never been away from home for a single night, except for those visits to Uncle Ike's. He was now in a strange place among strangers, a small, shy, scared boy of about thirteen or fourteen. He missed Mayann, he missed Mama Lucy, he missed the people of the Perdido Street neighborhood with whom he had grown up. So homesick was he that for two days he could not speak to anybody, could not even eat anything.

But finally on the third day, as he sat down in front of his plate of beans, his hunger overcame him, and he began to eat. The food made him feel more cheerful, and that night he began, in his shy way, to make friends.

Very quickly thereafter Louis began to adjust to living in the Waifs' Home. Once he got over being homesick, he realized that the Waifs' Home was in a lot of ways better than his own home. True, the food was very limited, but there was enough of it, and he never had to worry if it would be there. True, the clothes the school gave him were worn and faded, but they were clean and neat. So was the dormitory room he lived in; so were the kitchen and the grounds. Life back in Perdido Street had been disorderly, with fights, drunks, bands playing, people coming and going in the streets at all hours, and Mayann disappearing from time to time. In the Waifs' Home things were done on schedule in a regular fashion. And it began to occur to Louis that he *liked* being in the Waifs' Home. Here he had shoes, clean clothes, steady meals; here there was somebody to look after him.

And here, most important of all, there was a band. It was not unusual for an institution of this kind to have a band. For one thing, people felt that music helped to civilize wayward boys. For another, bands could play in the street and help to raise money for the orphanage.

The band at the Waifs' Home was like others at similar places. It consisted mostly of brass instruments, such as cornets, trombones, and tubas, along with a drum or two and tambourines. The band was not a jazz band, but mainly played marches, hymns, and old favorites like "Old Folks at Home," and "Maryland, My Maryland." They were pretty rough, these bands, because the boys were mostly beginners. They played out of tune a lot and missed many notes; but, still, the music was lively and energetic.

The band master was Peter Davis, a tall, thin black man. Davis knew something about music, but he was not a thoroughly trained music teacher. However, he did the best he could with his boys in order to produce a reasonably good band. Louis wanted desperately to be invited to join the band. Day after day he would come into the room where they were rehearsing. He would sit in a corner, listening and saying nothing, but hoping that Mr. Davis would ask him to join. From time to time Davis would glance at him, but he never asked Louis to come into the band. Why? What was wrong? Louis was sure he could do as well as any of the other boys. Why must he sit and wait? Did Davis think he was a bad kid, just because he came from the roughest neighborhood in the city?

For several weeks things went on this way. Louis grew increasingly desperate at being locked out of something he wanted so badly. Still Davis said nothing. It was Captain Jones who finally got Louis involved with music. A woman named Mrs. Spriggins came out to the Waifs' Home from time to time to conduct a choir where she taught the boys to sing. Captain Jones put Louis in the choir. And then one day, not long after, Peter Davis came over to Louis as he sat by himself in the corner watching rehearsal and asked him if he wanted to join the band.

Louis never knew why Davis had kept him out so long or why he had changed his mind about letting him join. But he was overjoyed, and he didn't ask questions. His joy turned a little sour, however, when Davis handed him a tambourine instead of a cornet or trombone. But Davis had a reason for his choice. Among blacks of New Orleans it was the custom to start beginners on rhythm instruments, like drums or tambourines, to give them a feeling for playing the beat accurately, with each note exactly in the right place. Louis swallowed his disappointment and sat in with the band, tapping the tambourine to the time. For him it was easy; he had been listening to ragtime and marches all his life. He had grown up with rhythmic music and knew how to play a clean, accurate beat.

Louis's chagrin at being given a tambourine was mitigated somewhat by the uniform he now had. It consisted of a gabardine coat, white pants turned up at the bottom, black stockings, sneakers, and a white cap. The uniform had been worn by many boys and was worn and faded; but it was the first time in his life Louis had had any sort of uniform, and he was proud to wear it.

The band rehearsed several times a week and practiced marching on the drill ground as well. From time to time, when Peter Davis thought he had a few numbers well enough rehearsed for a public performance, he would march the band out of the Waifs' Home and down dusty roads into the city proper. Here the members would set up on street corners and play for bystanders, with one of the boys passing a hat for pennies, nickels, and dimes. For Louis, it was a great feeling to be part of a real band, playing in his own city, even if he was only playing a tambourine.

Davis quickly realized that Louis had a good sense of rhythm. He moved him to the bass drum. Louis learned to play that with ease, and, not long after, Davis gave Louis his first horn. This was what was called a mellophone, or peck horn—what we today usually call an alto horn. It was an important switch for Louis, because the alto horn is not very different from the cornet. It has valves that are fingered the same as the cornet's, and it is blown almost exactly the same way, except that the mouthpiece is slightly larger.

Now Louis was faced with a real challenge. Like a lot of the boys in the band he could not read music. He had to work out a harmony part to the tunes by ear. And here is where all that singing he did in his quartet proved to be valuable. Just by hearing the melody, Louis knew immediately which notes made a good harmony part. All he had to do then was to find them on his horn. At first this took a little doing, but as he became familiar with the horn, he began to know how to play any note he could "hear" in his head. Within weeks he was easily playing harmony parts to the melodies the band played.

Peter Davis realized that he had something special in Louis Armstrong, and when the boy who played the bugle to wake the boys up and call them to dinner was discharged, Davis made Louis the bugler. A bugle has a mouthpiece like a cornet's and is blown the same way. The only difference is that the bugle has no valves and, as a consequence, cannot play all the notes for a complete scale. But that didn't matter; Louis had learned cornet fingering from playing the alto horn. Now on the bugle he was learning a cornet *embouchure*—that is to say, the set of the lips and tongue used in blowing a brass instrument. He was ready to play a cornet. Soon Peter Davis gave him one and put him up front in the band, playing the melody, or "lead," as musicians call it. Louis was now at the top of the band, admired by the rest as one of the best among them. It made him smile just to think of it.

Playing regularly in a band gave Louis an understanding of what music is and how it works. He was beginning to see, for one thing, why a beautiful melody could move people. There was a "meaning" in melody. It actually seemed to say something that could almost be put into words. Some music, Louis discovered, danced along cheerfully, as if it were being whistled by somebody walking along a pretty road on a sunny morning. Other music spoke of somber things, of sadness and death. Some melodies were thoughtful and wondered why things must be so; still others shouted hoarsely with excitement.

Melody, Louis discovered, was full of things, and he was discovering that he could make it say what he wanted to say. Music could be a way of expressing his feelings—cheerful or sad or pensive.

But Louis was also learning something else that he should not have been learning, although he didn't realize it. Peter Davis tried to do the best with the boys under his direction, but, as was usually the case with poor blacks of his time and place, he had never had a great deal of music instruction himself. He did not recognize, therefore, that his favorite pupil was developing some very bad habits in playing. For one thing, Louis was using too much of the red, soft part of his upper lip in his *embouchure*, instead of trying as much as possible to place the horn on the outer, tougher part. For another, he was pressing the mouthpiece too hard against his lips, especially the upper one, when he played the high notes in the upper register. This last is an especially common failing among poorly trained brass players, who find it easier to reach the high notes if they bear down on the upper lip. Doing this can cause all sorts of damage to the lips and even the teeth. Worse, it prevents young players from developing the strength in their lips that would allow them to reach the upper register without pressure. But Louis had no one to point any of this out to him, and it would be ominous for his future.

Louis was also discovering something else about himself at the Waifs' Home. This was that he could be funny, that he could make people laugh. He was "jokified," as the boys said. Years later Peter Davis said:

> I remember Louis used to walk funny with his feet pointing out and at the first note of music he'd break into comedy dances. He could sing real well as a boy, too, even though his voice was coarse. I'd play the horn and he'd dance, then when I'd put my horn down he'd pick it up and start playing it.

This, too, would have consequences for the future.

It is not surprising, then, that Louis was happy in the Waifs' Home. He had people to look after him, the other boys liked him, and he was a leader among them. It was a good feeling—a big improvement over the rough, uncertain life he had lived with Mayann on Perdido Street.

It all seemed to come together one day when the band, with Louis in front playing cornet lead, paraded out of the Waifs' Home, down that dusty road into the city, and through the streets of New Orleans into his old neighborhood. The band stopped at Perdido Street and played, and all the hustlers gathered around to listen and point out their own Little Louis in his uniform, blowing his cornet. As he stood there in the front of the band he could hardly believe that it was he, Louis Armstrong, standing in front of the band, just as he had seen his heroes Bunk Johnson, Buddie Petit, and the others do so many times; and his heart swelled within him. He was a musician, and it was all he would ever want to be.

As much as Louis liked the Waifs' Home, after he had been there for eighteen months or so, he began to chafe a little. Now going on sixteen, he felt that he was a grown-up, or anyway would very shortly be one. He didn't want to be a boy any longer. It was time, he told himself, to get out of the Home, to stop drilling with wooden guns and going to bed when somebody blew a bugle, and to take on a man's responsibilities.

The problem was the indefinite sentence Judge Wilson had given him, which meant that it was up to Wilson to decide when he could be released. He could try running away. It was easy enough, and other boys had done it. But they had usually been caught quickly, brought back, and given a solid whipping. It wasn't worth it.

Mayann came out to the Waifs' Home to visit Louis sometimes, and he talked it over with her. Could she persuade Judge Wilson to let Louis go home? It seemed doubtful; Mayann didn't have a very good record as a mother, although that didn't matter to Louis.

Suddenly, Louis's father, Willie Armstrong, stepped in. Louis was astonished that his father wanted to do something for him. He had very mixed feelings about him. One part of him wanted his father to love him, to care for him, to do things with him. Another part of him was angry at his father for neglecting him for so many years. So he was somewhat confused by his father's surprising intervention.

It soon became clear why his father was interested. Willie had two boys by his second wife; they were Louis's half brothers. Willie wanted somebody in the house full time to baby-sit for the children, so that his wife could take a job. Money was scarce and there were a lot of mouths to feed.

Leaving the Waifs' Home to become a baby-sitter for his half brothers was not Louis's idea of becoming a man. But it was a way out of the Home, and he agreed. So Willie Armstrong went to Judge Wilson and explained that if the judge would release Louis, he would take him in. Although Willie had been a far worse parent to Louis than had Mayann, he had a steady job and an orderly home. To Judge Wilson it looked like a much better situation for Louis, and he released Louis into the custody of his father.

So Louis became a baby-sitter. Not only did he have to look after the two boys, whom he found argumentative, but he also had to cook their meals, clean up after them, and do the regular housekeeping besides. Far from becoming a man, he had been turned into a domestic drudge. Once again he chafed.

He had hardly been there more than a few months, however, when his stepmother, Gertrude Armstrong, gave birth to a third child, a little girl. She could now no longer work and would have to stay home anyway. Willie Armstrong didn't need a baby-sitter anymore, and he didn't need another mouth to feed, so why bother to keep Louis around? He told Louis he could go back to Perdido Street and live with Mayann.

It was not very friendly for his father to send him away abruptly, and Louis knew it. But he was already bitter enough about his father and expected nothing from him anyway. He was glad to leave, and he went back to Perdido Street, his heart growing lighter with each step. As he climbed the stairs to the balcony that led to his house, he was happy finally to be home.

Mayann and Mama Lucy were as happy to see him as he was to be back. He had changed, they could see; he was no longer a boy, even though he still was barefoot and wearing short pants. He looked like a man to them.

There was a third member of the household, too. One of Louis's cousins, the fourteen-year-old daughter of Uncle Ike, had given birth to a little boy. According to the family, she had been seduced by an old white man who lived not far from the neighborhood, who was always after young black girls. People had told Uncle Ike that he should sue the old man, but Uncle Ike knew that was hopeless. A black man could not expect to get justice from a white judge in a white court against a white man. He was helpless.

Flora named her little boy Clarence. And then, not long after, she died. What was to be done with the baby? Uncle Ike had to be away all day sweating on the docks to feed his family. He hardly needed another mouth to feed. So Mayann had taken in the baby. Uncle Ike had looked after Louis and Mama Lucy often enough when Mayann had been off on a spree with her boyfriends. It was time Mayann did something for Uncle Ike.

But very quickly Louis realized that Clarence was going to be his responsibility, too. Mama Lucy had always looked up to him to take care of her when Mayann disappeared, and Mayann herself had counted on Louis's helping out with things right from the time he was seven or so and had come back to live with her. He had always borne part of the responsibility for the family, and now he saw that the two women—his mother and his sister—were expecting him to be the man of the house. He had become, in a curious way, the father of himself.

Louis didn't mind. In fact, he was proud of being a man, proud of being responsible for the family. The first thing was to get a job. He wanted to work as a musician. But he knew he was not good enough. It was one thing to play lead cornet in a boys' band; it would be quite another to play in a blues band in a honky-tonk for the hustlers and their women, who had ideas about how they wanted their music played and no qualms about letting the band know. He needed to practice, to learn, and for that he needed a cornet. But that was still impossible. With a family of four to feed, there was no way he could save up the ten dollars or so a secondhand cornet would cost, even if Mayann were working, too. Money didn't stay in Mayann's hands very long; the honky-tonks at both ends of the block were too tempting.

He went looking for work, and shortly he found himself a job on a coal cart. Over the next three years Louis would have various kinds of odd jobs: delivering milk, working on the docks as a stevedore like Uncle Ike, painting houses; but most of the time he worked on coal carts.

The carts were wooden and rough, held a ton of coal, and were drawn by mules. Louis would report to the coal yard every morning, hitch up a mule to his cart, and shovel a ton of coal into it. Then he would climb up on the cart and drive it around to the customers' houses, where he would shovel the coal into a heap into the customers' backyards. He was paid fifteen cents for each load, and he could manage only five or six loads a day because he was small. Sometimes a customer would tip him a nickel or a dime extra; sometimes they would give him a pork or fish sandwich. It was a rare day when he made as much as a dollar, and some days he made less than seventy-five cents.

It was tough, dirty work. But Louis accepted it; what else could he do? He was poor, he was black, and this was the way that poor black people lived their lives. Why should he be any different? He was learning a lesson Mayann had taught and many people have to learn—there was no point in constantly being angry about things you couldn't change. He couldn't change the color of his skin, and he couldn't change the way whites treated black people. He had better just shrug it off, he decided, and get on with his life as best he could within the limits the world had set for him.

Besides, he had something to keep him going: his dream of becoming a musician. As he shoveled coal into his cart he could imagine himself sitting in one of the tonks next to the piano, playing the blues for the customers to dance to. He could imagine himself parading at the head of a street band in a bright red and blue uniform, blowing out the lead on some pretty melody like "Listen to the Mockingbird," or a stirring march like "Stars and Stripes Forever," with its brisk phrases. He could imagine himself in the balcony in Funky Butt Hall high above the dancers, playing the ragtime he had heard so often through the cracks in the wall. He could even imagine himself in a blue and white uniform on the deck of one of the beautiful riverboats, all shiny with new paint. He would play the newest dance tunes while the boat pulled away from the New Orleans docks and headed up the Mississippi for those glamorous cities he had heard about but never seen and could hardly envision: Memphis, St. Louis, Davenport, and even St. Paul, over a thousand miles away in a strange country of pines and cool lakes.

And when he climbed up on the coal cart to drive his load to the next customer, he would sing those melodies he loved, sometimes jumping into the harmony parts he knew for a few bars before switching back to the melodies. At these times the world fell away from him and the coal, the cart, the mule disappeared; there was nothing but music around him.

In the evenings, when he had washed the coal dust off and eaten his supper of rice and beans and the chicken or chops he could now afford, he would leave the house and wander through the neighborhood, swarming with men and women out for a good time. Through the streets he would go, stopping at this tonk and that one—Matranga's, Joe Segretto's, Kid Brown's—looking for music. Not all the tonks had music, and even those that did might not have a band every night. So Louis would prowl the streets, looking.

Usually he found some music. Sometimes it would be just a pianist, sometimes a guitarist and a drummer, sometimes a clarinet or cornet accompanied by drums and guitar or piano. But always they would play the blues, low and slow, filled with bent and twisted notes, with the drum banging and the clarinet or cornet growling.

Louis, now sixteen, would go in, order a great mug of beer for a nickel, and stand in the smoky atmosphere watching the dancers and listening to the band play. He loved it all, and yet it was painful, too, because he yearned to be up there with the musicians, playing the blues and ragtime.

At some point during this time Louis began to strike up a friendship with a man named Black Benny Williams. Benny Williams was a drummer, but he was also a hustler, one of the hardest of the toughs who hung around Louis's neighborhood. Nobody crossed Benny Williams, and nobody told him what to do.

When Benny was flush with money, he wore Stetson hats and box-backed coats with sharp creases pressed into them. When he was broke he pawned his suit and wore old clothes.

Once a policeman came to arrest Benny for something he had done. The policeman said, "Come on, Benny, I'm taking you in." Benny had just gotten his best suit out of pawn; he was looking fine and feeling good. "Oh, no," he said. "I just got my suit out of pawn, and I'm going to wear it for a day before I go to jail."

So the policeman spun Benny around and grabbed him by the seat of his pants with one hand and by the collar with the other. He started to push Benny toward the jail. But Benny twisted around in the muddy streets and just walked off, dragging the policeman down the street through the mud until he gave up and let go.

When Benny was low on money, he would sometimes go around to the tonks and collect pistols to sell. He would just walk up to somebody and say, "Let's see your gun," and when the person showed it to him Benny would say, "Okay, I'm taking it." Nobody ever argued, and when Benny had collected a few—fur-handled ones, silver-plated ones—he would take them around to the pawn shop and sell them for a dollar apiece to have some money for drinks and gambling.

Benny was famous around Louis's neighborhood, and Louis admired and envied him. Benny was big and tough; Louis was small and shy, and he wished he were more like Benny. So, when Louis happened to see Benny standing at a bar in a tonk talking to someone and drinking a mug of beer, he would walk up to the bar and stand beside Benny—just a little bit off—and order a mug of beer for himself. Then he would wait, and after a while Benny would notice him standing there. He would say something like, "Hiya, kid." And Louis would say, "Hi, Benny," and offer to buy him a mug of beer.

After a while Benny realized that this short teenager was tagging around after him. Louis admired him, he saw; and he began to take a liking to Louis.

Striking up a friendship with Black Benny Williams was important for Louis. Louis was small, and it was a very tough neighborhood. But once word got around that Black Benny was keeping an eye on Louis, nobody would dare bother him. Furthermore, Louis was shy and Black Benny emphatically was not. As a drummer he knew a lot of musicians and could open doors for Louis. But there was more to it than that. Louis had never had a father to look after him, to protect him from the neighborhood toughs, to find a way to get him a cornet when he was desperate for one. Benny seemed to Louis just the sort of father he always wished he'd had—a strong, tough man who was afraid of nobody and whom everybody respected. So Louis adopted Benny as his father. Of course Louis didn't think it out as clearly as this; he just did what he felt. But that was the effect of it.

With Benny behind him Louis felt a little bolder

about attempting to become a musician. He told Benny that he was determined to get a horn, to learn to play. There was not much Benny could do about teaching Louis music, but he had many friends among the musicians who played in the tonks and the street parades, and it was easy enough for him to say, "Let Little Louis sit in." Nobody would refuse to do Black Benny a favor.

Louis began sitting in at the tonks in his neighborhood, especially at Matranga's and Joe Segretto's. In many of the tonks the musicians worked twelve-hour stretches, with few breaks along the way. At Segretto's the music went around the clock, twenty-four hours a day, at times, with different combinations of musicians taking turns. The musicians were always glad to get a break to have a drink or a sandwich, and they didn't mind letting people sit in, as long as they could play a little.

At this point in his career, Louis was not really good enough to play even the rough music of the tonks. He had heard the blues all his life, and he quickly worked out a way of playing a simple version, enough to get by. Beyond this he knew only two or three of the ragtime tunes that the hustlers and the women in the tonks liked. The songs he had learned at the Waifs' Home were hymns, marches, and the old favorites like "Home, Sweet Home"—not exactly what the people in tonks wanted to hear.

But even though Louis was not really good enough to sit in, the musicians let him do it anyway, because he was eager and likable and they didn't mind taking a break. Besides, they didn't want it getting back to Black Benny that they had refused to let Louis come up and blow.

Louis had to borrow a cornet from whichever player he relieved. He still could not afford a cornet of his own. This made it impossible to sit in with bands that didn't have a cornetist. Worse, it made it impossible for him to practice at home. But he was determined, and night after night he walked through the hot, raw atmosphere of the neighborhood, looking for a place to sit in, even if only for one number. And gradually, painfully, a bit at a time, he began to improve. Sixteen years old, he was basically responsible for supporting his family. He worked ten hours a day, six days a week, shoveling coal. He had to figure out music for himself on borrowed instruments. His primary guide in life was a hustler who wanted only to drink, gamble, wear fancy clothes, and carry on with women. And yet out of desire and sheer will, Louis was making himself into a musician.

# CHAPTER FIVE

About 1914 and 1915, when Louis Armstrong was serving his apprenticeship in the honky-tonks, people around New Orleans were beginning to be aware that a new kind of music was in the air. It had a snappy beat that made you want to dance, and it was filled with growls and shouts and strange twisted notes. It was a lot like ragtime, and a little like those curious blues you could hear blacks on the levees playing on whining guitars, or coming out of the honky-tonks, if you were willing to go into that neighborhood. Not everybody knew about this new music, but people who went out in the evenings to dance or drink or gamble couldn't escape hearing it. Some people were calling it "jazzing the music up."

Even the musicians themselves were not quite sure what the new music was. As a matter of fact, some of them didn't like it. The ones with better musical training especially considered it rough and dirty and sometimes called it "stink music." But a lot of musicians, particularly the young ones, thought it was wonderful. They wanted to play it, and they did so whenever they got the chance.

Where did jazz come from? Nobody really knows the

answer, but it is clear enough that it grew out of some combination of ragtime and the blues. Blues and ragtime used quite different types of rhythms. Musicians who were playing both kinds of music, especially in the tonks and the dance halls of Louis Armstrong's neighborhood, began to mix these rhythms in ways that were extremely subtle and still not well understood. They also began adding the bent "blue notes" to their rags, until their ragtime began to grow into something new. Then, when they had discovered this new way of playing rags, they began to play other kinds of music, like marches and popular songs, the same way, too. And by somewhere around 1913 or 1914 or 1915, the music we today call jazz was coming into its first maturity.

Thus, jazz and Louis Armstrong grew up together. When he was born it did not exist; the blues were only just coming into being, and ragtime was just becoming widely popular across the United States. By the time he went into the Waifs' Home, ragtime was a great fad not only in the United States, but in Europe as well; the first blues songs were being published as sheet music; and the new jazz music was breaking off from its ragtime parent. When he began prowling around the streets of his neighborhood, looking for places to sit in, ragtime was a huge industry, the blues were spreading throughout the South, and jazz had become, like Louis, an independent being.

Black Benny Williams did not live to see much of this transformation, however. Around this time he got rough once too often. He got into a fight with one of his girlfriends, and she shot him. Louis said years later that Benny was so tough that he lived for a week with the bullet in his heart. But even Benny was not tough enough to survive that.

Louis was hurt by the death of Benny Williams, but he had reached the point where he could stand on his own feet a little better. He was becoming a more capable cornetist. People were beginning to recognize him as a competent blues player. He still could only play a few tunes—lack of a cornet to practice on held him back—but week by week, month by month, he was painfully expanding his repertoire.

What he needed now was a cornet. And this he got quite unexpectedly when he was about seventeen and had been playing in the tonks for a year or so. He happened to run into Charles, for whom he had sold papers years before. Charles was now a man, with a little money in his pocket. Louis told him about his determination to become a musician, and Charles simply lent Louis ten dollars for a horn. Louis was so excited he could hardly wait to thank Charles before dashing off to the pawn shops along South Rampart Street to find a horn. After a search he found a battered cornet, dented, tarnished, and with a hole in the bell, that was priced at ten dollars. Appropriately enough, it was a Tonk Brothers model, a brand nobody has heard of since.

Battered and discolored as it was, it looked like gold to Louis. Now he could practice. Now he could sit in at tonks where they didn't have a cornet player. He could even sit beside other cornet players and try to "catch" their notes as they played, by following their fingering.

Now that he had a horn of his own, Louis's progress speeded up. He began to learn more tunes, increase his stamina, widen his range, and improve his sound. The musicians in the tonks, and the managers who ran them, realized that Louis was becoming a real musician. He was by no means the best around, but he could get by, and they began using him as a substitute. When a cornet player was sick or tired or just didn't want to work, somebody would say, "Send for Little Louis." Louis would drop everything and hurry around to the tonk. He would sometimes play all night and then have to go out to work on his coal cart without any rest. It didn't matter; he would do anything for the chance to play.

He knew he was finally accepted when the manager of Henry Matranga's asked him to become the regular cornetist with the house band. It was just a little rough three-piece band, with a man called Boogus on piano and a drummer named Garbee. The pay was a dollar a night, and tips might run to another twenty-five cents. The hours were long—many times Louis got only two hours' sleep before he had to report to the coal yard. But he was now a professional musician— not a very good one yet, but one whom the other musicians were keeping an eye on. Little Louis, many of them said, was a comer. So night after night he would sit in front of the piano and drums in Matranga's, breathing the thick smoke, smelling the raw smell of spilled beer and whiskey, listening to the shouts and whoops of the dancers and the gamblers in the back room, watching the hustlers, the hard stevedores, and the cotton pickers dance with their women. In front of him, frequently, there were fights. At times guns would suddenly appear out of back pockets and knives out of boots; there would be shouting, while Louis and the other musicians dropped to the floor. Occasionally blood would stain somebody's clothes, soak into the sawdust, and the police would arrive with an ambulance. It was a dirty, rough, coarse, and dangerous place; but there was nowhere else in the world Louis would rather be.

Louis was now learning something else about music. He had always loved melody, even as a child. He had loved the turns of it, the curves and scrolls and saw-toothed shapes in it; he had loved the way the melody seemed to talk to you. But now he was discovering in ragtime, and even more in this new music that people were beginning to call jazz, something in the rhythm, a lilt, a swing, that excited people. It was not anything that he could put into words, but he could feel it when it was played. And he was discovering that he, too, could capture some of that lilt, that swing, in his own playing. Not always—sometimes the music came out flat-footed, leaden; it refused to leap off the ground. But sometimes the music would grow light and fly, and he would grow light, too, and smile inside.

Louis was improving rapidly, but he was far from the best jazz cornetist in the city. That title, most people who knew about such things agreed, belonged to a big, heavyset man, with one bad eye, named Joseph "King" Oliver. Oliver played with a band led by trombonist Edward Ory, who was always called "Kid." Ory was considered the best jazz trombonist in New Orleans, and his band was accounted the finest one going. Kid Ory was a cheerful, outgoing man and a responsible leader who saw to it that the men showed up for jobs on time, played the way he wanted them to, and were paid well—at least as well as a black musician in New Orleans could expect to be paid. Ory's band scorned the stink bands in the tonks. It played in dance halls, and it frequently played at the New Orleans country club, expensive restaurants, and even at private parties in the homes of wealthy whites.

King Oliver was a different sort of man from Ory. He was tough, shrewd, tight with his money, and liked to be the dominant man in all situations. Oliver drank little, but he loved to eat. He would eat a whole chicken at a meal, or a half dozen hamburgers, with a whole pie for dessert, and wash it down with a full pot of coffee. He was a homebody, too. He liked to stay with his wife and stepdaughter on evenings when he had no job, and take things easy.

But basically Oliver was a tough man who made things go the way he wanted. Louis Armstrong was attracted to him, just as he had been attracted to Benny Williams. Oliver was, again, a forceful man much admired by the blacks of the city—just the sort of man a boy would want for a father.

Louis set out to attract King Oliver's attention. The Ory band, like many New Orleans bands, played a lot of parades for funerals, advertising, or social clubs celebrating an occasion. A musician on parade could not, of course, carry his instrument case with him. He needed somebody to bring it along for him. Sometimes the musicians' wives or girlfriends would carry their cases, but it was also a custom for boys or young aspiring musicians to carry cases for the players they most admired. Sometimes there would be competition among them to see who got to carry the instrument case of a popular musician.

Louis began making a point of finding out what parades Oliver was playing. He would get there early and ask Oliver to let him carry the case. Oliver usually said yes.

Oliver's wife Stella frequently came along on these parades. Louis struck up conversations with her, too. Sometimes he would run errands for her. And in this fashion Louis got to know King Oliver and his wife. Just as Benny Williams had done, Oliver took a liking to Louis. He began showing Louis things about playing the cornet, helping him learn tunes, giving him advice about his style. Sometimes Stella would invite Louis around to the house for a meal.

After Oliver had heard Louis play he realized that he was talented. Inevitably, he began letting Louis sit in for him occasionally when he wanted a break. And finally, Oliver began recommending Louis for jobs he could not take himself.

J azz was invented in New Orleans. It is hard to say why it happened there and not anywhere else. But it had to do with a lot of things coming together there that didn't happen quite the same way in other places in the South. In any case, the music was too interesting and exciting to stay confined to New Orleans. During the years after 1910 tourists visiting the city heard this new ragtime and began talking about it when they went back home. New Orleans, remember, was a good town for tourists, and as they were out for a good time, they usually went to places where they were bound to hear the latest music.

During this same period there was a great flood of blacks out of the South into the cold, industrial cities of the North. Blacks were leaving the South because conditions in the North were a little better, and especially because, during World War I, there were plenty of jobs for blacks in factories in New York, Detroit, Chicago, and other northern cities. The situation for blacks in the North was hardly perfect: There was a great deal of race prejudice there. Many whites would beat up blacks, or actually bomb their homes, if they tried to move into white neighborhoods, and in general blacks had to take the hardest jobs for the lowest pay. Nonetheless, things were better than in the South. Blacks in the North could go to schools, and even colleges. Although most spent their lives doing hard physical labor, some did better for themselves, and a few even managed to become bankers, lawyers, doctors. In their own neighborhoods, like New York's Harlem or Chicago's South Side Black Belt, they could relax and breathe freely among their own people.

This flow of blacks northward carried along with it a certain number of musicians, especially blues players who could play the music the immigrants, often homesick in the big, strange cities, remembered from down South.

Thus, through both blacks and whites, word of jazz began to spread out from New Orleans. Even as early as 1911, a fine New Orleans cornet player named Freddy Keppard went on a theater tour with a jazz band from back home called the Original Creole Orchestra. Other black musicians began working up and down the towns of the Gulf Coast, going well into Texas.

But blacks were not alone in playing jazz. The young white musicians around New Orleans, many of them teenagers, had been hearing the new hot music growing out of ragtime right from the beginning. As early as 1912, when Louis Armstrong was about to go into the Waifs' Home, young whites were trying to play this hot music, this advanced ragtime. They got the idea very quickly, and although it was some time before they were able to play as well as the blacks, they were not far behind.

In 1915 and 1916 some of these white musicians traveled north to Chicago to present the new music in cabarets there. These bands were a great success, and in 1917 one of them, the Original Dixieland Jazz Band, went to New York to play at a famous restaurant called Reisenweber's. They were an even greater success and, shortly thereafter, were asked by Victor Record Company to record. These first jazz records were an enormous hit. Within months the Original Dixieland Jazz Band was famous, and all across the United States aspiring musicians, many of them teenagers, were trying to learn to play jazz. By 1918 a jazz boom was on. There was a demand for it everywhere, for dancing or just listening.

Very quickly the musicians from New Orleans who could play jazz, especially the blacks, realized that there was a great opportunity waiting for them in the North. New Orleans was a small city. Although it had famous entertainment districts, it simply did not have the numbers of dance cabarets or nightclubs to be found in New York, Chicago, and Los Angeles. Pay was much higher in the North. In New Orleans a musician might earn a dollar or two a night; in Chicago pay could be fifty or seventy-five dollars a week.

So the jazz musicians began to flow north. And in 1918 King Oliver joined the migration. That left Kid Ory without a cornetist, and what was more natural than for Oliver to recommend his young admirer, Louis Armstrong, for the job? Kid Ory agreed that Louis was ready, and he went around to see him. At the time Louis Armstrong was still wearing short pants. "Get yourself a pair of long pants," Ory said, "and be ready to play at eight o'clock." Louis got his long pants and was so excited and eager to play that he went to the job two hours early.

Louis was now a member of the best jazz band in New Orleans. He had come a long way in four years, but he had worked hard for it, struggling to get a foothold in the tonks, going to work on the coal cart after playing all night at Matranga's, taking advantage of every chance to improve, to learn more. Nobody had given him anything; he had had to fight for everything.

The Ory band mainly played dances. They were frequently held in tough dance halls for blacks, like Funky Butt Hall, but the band also spend a good deal of its time playing for whites. It played at Tom Anderson's, a popular restaurant in the white entertainment district, and in a cabaret nearby called Pete Lala's. It also played occasionally for parties at the New Orleans Country Club, which was for whites only, and at some of the city's best-known restaurants.

The work was somewhat irregular, however. The band usually had jobs on the weekends and at times during the week, but there were gaps. And because the pay was not high, Louis continued to work on the coal cart to make sure the family had a steady income.

It was hard to get up in the morning and go to work when he had been out in a smoky dance hall playing until three in the morning, but Louis was young and healthy, and he managed, always looking forward to the day when he could be a full-time musician.

That time came a year after he joined the Ory band. In 1919 Kid Ory began to suffer spells of coughing. His doctor told him that he was having trouble with his lungs and ought to move to a dryer climate. A New Orleans jazz pianist named Jelly Roll Morton had gone out to Los Angeles not long before, and word had come back that Jelly was getting plenty of work for his band there. Ory decided to go to California. His band broke up, and once again Louis was out of work. He managed to pick up odd jobs playing parades, or working in dance halls with bands of his own made up of friends he had made among the musicians, but there was nothing steady.

Meanwhile Ory, out in California, rapidly regained his health. He quickly discovered that Jelly Roll Morton had been right; people were excited by the new hot jazz music coming out of New Orleans, and there would be plenty of work for a good jazz band. So Ory sent a telegram back to New Orleans to a musician he knew there, asking him to bring some jazz players out. The musician knew that Armstrong had played with Ory before, and he asked Louis to go out to Los Angeles to join him again.

Louis wavered. It would be a great opportunity to see some of the world, make more money than he ever could in New Orleans, and perhaps even get his name around a little.

But Louis was shy. He had never been more than a few miles from New Orleans, and he had spent most of his life in a small, familiar neighborhood among people he knew. Los Angeles, Chicago, St. Louis—these were strange, foreign places. Perhaps people in California were different and wouldn't like him. Perhaps he wouldn't know what to do, how to behave. While Ory waited impatiently for the band to come, Louis thought it over. Finally he said no, he would stay in New Orleans. He hated to admit it to himself, but he didn't have the nerve.

Yet the fact that he had been chosen to go to California was a clear sign that Louis's reputation, among musicians at least, was growing. There were a number of other good jazz cornetists around New Orleans—but Louis had been picked.

With his reputation growing, it is not surprising that he awakened the interest of a band leader named Fate Marable. Marable had first heard Louis play in a dance hall with the Ory band. He was a pianist, but more important, he was in charge of bands for one of the riverboats owned by the Streckfus Line.

These big old paddle-wheel boats had once been the fastest means of transportation in the central United States. They roamed everywhere in the Mississippi River system, from New Orleans to St. Paul, from Cincinnati to Omaha, carrying passengers and freight. But when the railroads were built across the country after the Civil War, the riverboats became outmoded and gradually disappeared. By the time Louis was born they were almost out of business.

One of the companies that suffered thus was the Streckfus Line, based in St. Louis. In order to save their company, the Streckfus people decided to turn some of their riverboats into floating dance halls. They knew that people living in little towns along the Mississippi did not have much by way of entertainment. So they refurbished two of their boats, giving them spanking new coats of paint and gilt designs stenciled on the sides, and hired bands to play for dancing. At first the bands were small, consisting of a piano and violin, but gradually they expanded until, by the time Louis Armstrong was playing with Kid Ory, they consisted of eight or ten pieces playing full arrangements of popular songs.

In summer, beginning about May, the riverboats started up the river from New Orleans. They would pull into the landings of towns along the way while Marable played the calliope, a huge steam organ that could be heard for miles around. The townspeople would come aboard, carrying picnic baskets full of sandwiches, cakes, pies, wine, and beer. The boat would travel upriver for a couple of hours and return around eleven o'clock at night. In the morning the boat would set out for the next town along the way. Sometimes the boats would be gone until fall, traveling all the way up to St. Paul, Minnesota.

Going out to dance, eat, and drink in the cool evening

river breezes was a very pleasant thing to do on a hot summer's night, and the riverboats proved to be very popular. In the winter, the boats would stay in New Orleans and make short side trips on Friday and Saturday nights and on Sunday afternoons.

In fall, 1918, Fate Marable asked Louis Armstrong if he would like to start working in his band on one of the riverboats. Louis was an odd choice for Marable, for his bands had arrangements of music to read, and Louis could hardly read music. But Marable wanted Louis anyway, because even if Louis couldn't read, he was as good a hot jazz player as anybody in New Orleans.

Louis was excited by the idea of playing on the riverboats, but nervous, too. Playing on the riverboats was one of the top jobs for a black or white musician in New Orleans. The pay was good, the quality of musicianship was high, the hours were shorter than at dances, and you got to see a lot of the world. On the other hand, the Streckfus people were strict: They wanted the music just so, and sometimes a ship's captain would time the band with a stopwatch to make sure that the tempos were right. Furthermore, the musicians had to read arrangements; the Streckfus bands played only a few improvised jazz numbers each night.

It worried Louis, because he could only read music a little. But Marable told him not to worry; he could learn to read what was needed. The riverboats had trained a lot of New Orleans musicians. And so Louis accepted the job. He might not have accepted, had it been the summer season, with the boat going a thousand miles up the river to those strange, faraway places like St. Louis and St. Paul. But for the winter the boat would only be going a few miles upriver each trip and be back home again by midnight.

Playing on the riverboats would be, the musicians told him, like going to school. And it was. The band played for four hours each evening and rehearsed twice a week. Fortunately for Louis, there was another cornetist in the band, Joe Howard, who played the lead. Howard helped Louis a good deal. He was helped even more by the band's mellophone player, David Jones. Jones was an excellent all-around musician who played several instruments and was a quick sight reader. The other players called him "Professor" because of his musical knowledge. He took the time to show Louis what the little lines and dots on the page meant. At first Louis struggled, but by the end of the winter season he was getting the hang of it. So Marable asked Louis if he wanted to make the summer trip up the Mississippi.

Now Louis was ready to go. He would be among people he knew, in surroundings he was familiar with. For the next three years Louis worked on the riverboats, playing the long tours in the summer and the short weekend trips in the winter. The experience was invaluable. Playing regularly and being forced to play to a high standard by strict bosses made Louis work on all aspects of his musicianship—his endurance, range, speed, sight reading, intonation, general accuracy. When he started on the riverboats in 1918 he was a rough, if obviously gifted, young musician. When he left the riverboats after the 1921 summer season, he was an experienced professional who could read well and play competently any kind of music the job called for. He even knew some difficult operatic arias, which he later would use as showpieces.

When he wasn't working on the riverboats he played the usual dances, parades, and whatever other jobs came along. During this time he became close to a man who was to be his friend—although not without troubles—for the rest of his life.

That was Arthur Singleton, a drummer, who was known to everybody as Zutty. Zutty was just the sort of young man that Louis wished he were. Zutty was outgoing, assertive, and witty. He was a man people gathered around, and he usually took charge of things. Louis admired Zutty's likable swagger, and Zutty was even more admiring of Louis's musical abilities. Beginning about the time Kid Ory moved to Los Angeles, Louis and Zutty worked together off and on in clubs when Louis was not out on the riverboats.

They were working together in a cabaret on Orchard Street when a handsome, light-skinned black with sophisticated manners and an educated voice came into the club. He was not much older than the two New Orleanians, but he clearly came from an entirely different world than Louis and Zutty's rough black entertainment district. He listened to Louis play for a while, and then he came over and introduced himself. His name was Fletcher Henderson, and he was pianist and leader of a group that was touring the South with a singer named Ethel Waters. Henderson also was an executive at the first black-owned record company, Black Swan, located in New York. Neither Henderson nor Ethel Waters was yet known; but in time he would become leader of the most important black dance band in the country, and she would become a movie star.

Henderson was impressed with the way Louis played. He was willing to offer him an immediate job if he would join the group backing Ethel Waters on its tour. Louis asked if he could think about it. It was a great opportunity for him, for it could bring him to New York, the center of the music business. It might lead to all sorts of things, including recording for Black Swan. In the end he said he would go only if Henderson would take Zutty Singleton along, too. Henderson could not do that. He already had a drummer, and he couldn't leave that man stranded in New Orleans and take Zutty. So Louis turned the opportunity down. It was the old story: He was just nervous about going off to strange places with strangers.

He had now twice turned down important opportunities to advance his career. Other jazz musicians were leaving New Orleans to go north, where they were beginning to make records and play in important nightclubs and theaters, making names for themselves. But still Louis Armstrong stayed home in the obscurity of New Orleans where he felt comfortable.

Nonetheless, it was an indication of his growing musical abilities that he had been offered jobs by three bandleaders: Kid Ory, Fate Marable, and Fletcher Henderson. Louis, people were beginning to realize, was not just another good New Orleans jazz musician. He was going to be something special.

What was it about Louis's playing that caught the ear of other musicians and led these important bandleaders to offer him jobs? For one thing, Louis had a growing ability to put into his playing that lilt, that swing, that was so exciting a part of the new hot jazz. By holding back a little on this note, jumping in early on that one, so that many of the notes didn't land smack on the beat but came unexpectedly a little early or late, he made the music seem to leap along. Then, too, he didn't play his notes evenly, but accented some and passed lightly over others, so that music seemed to be alive, to breathe.

Besides this sense of swing, Louis was also developing an ability to add surprising little twists and turns to the melody, invented at the moment. Although the jazz musicians around Louis tended to play each song more or less the same way every time, they were increasingly taking liberties, embellishing the melody with little filigrees, or even changing whole phrases by working out new melodies that fit the basic harmonies of the tune. Louis, the other musicians were beginning to realize, had a marvelous ear for harmony and was able to invent especially exciting new bits of melody.

Up north in Chicago, word of Louis's development had reached King Oliver. King had quickly made himself a leader of a group of New Orleanian jazz players. His band had begun playing in Chicago, spent a year on the West Coast, and then, in April 1922, come back to Chicago to play at a black dance hall called Lincoln Gardens. Sometime shortly after his return, King Oliver decided he wanted Little Louis to come into the band to play second cornet. On a hot July day, as Louis was finishing a parade, he was handed a telegram from Oliver. This time, he realized, he would not be going off to play among strangers; he would be under the big, protective wing of Joe Oliver. And he wired Oliver that he would come.

he Chicago that was to be Louis Armstrong's home base for most of the next seven years was quite different from New Orleans. His hometown was a bit slow and easygoing. Chicago was tough and bustling. It was a major railroad junction and Great Lakes port, and through it flowed millions of dollars' worth of beef, corn, steel, manufactured goods, and almost everything else that flowed east to west, west to east, across America. It was busy getting rich.

Drawn to the good jobs that the city provided in flush times were thousands of new immigrants to America—Poles, Hungarians, Swedes, Italians, and many more. Large numbers of these people had settled in ethnic groups in Chicago's South Side district. Coming up from the South were also tens of thousands of blacks aiming for better jobs, a freer atmosphere, and a gayer life than they had back home in their shanties in the cotton fields. Over one hundred thousand blacks came to Chicago from the South in the 1920s alone.

They, too, settled in the South Side, creating what came to be called the Black Belt, a narrow area running lengthwise through the South Side. Here they built a neighborhood of their own, with an excellent black newspaper, the *Chicago Defender*, black doctors, black lawyers, shops where black clerks served black customers. Actually, most of the shops were owned by whites, who scooped off a lot of the money that blacks spent in the area, but at least in the South Side whites were not as omnipresent as they were in southern towns. There were parks where you would not see a white face, nightclubs and pool rooms that were entirely black. There was even the fancy Gold Coast: large, elegant houses along South Parkway, where a handful of wealthy blacks lived.

Chicago was an improvement over the South for blacks, but it was no paradise. Most blacks didn't live on the Gold Coast, but in ramshackle two-story wooden buildings, usually containing one apartment on each floor. Most of the South Side, in fact, was dirty and dilapidated. As elsewhere, blacks had to take the hardest, lowest-paying jobs, and they could not buy houses in white neighborhoods. Nonetheless, it was better than the South.

One other important aspect of Chicago in the 1920s was the fact that it was run to a considerable extent by gangsters. In 1920 laws prohibiting the sale of liquor had come into force all over the United States. However, people still wanted to drink, and very quickly gangs went into the business of selling illegal alcohol, which was smuggled in from Canada or made in hidden factories in warehouses and even apartment bathtubs. There was an enormous amount of money to be made from the sale of illegal alcohol, and all over the United States gangs fought for control of the business.

In Chicago, the gangs managed to buy off most of the city government. Police were under orders to look the other way when they spotted trucks carrying beer through the city or clubs selling it after it was delivered. Saloons operated openly in Chicago, and rival gangs fought with machine guns in the street to gain the upper hand.

These gangs didn't confine themselves to selling liquor. They also owned the nightclubs, cabarets, and saloons that sold the liquor and drugs, as well as gambling dives, brothels, and anything else illegal that would bring in money. A great many of these illegal activities were carried on in the South Side, especially in the Black Belt. Many whites felt that it really didn't matter what happened in black areas. Blacks were just animals, anyway, they said. And there grew up in the heart of the area, around State and Thirty-fifth streets, an entertainment district containing theaters, clubs, saloons, and cheap cellar dives of various sorts. These places were ostensibly for blacks, but in fact they also were meant to draw white customers, who had more money than blacks to spend. And every night into the Black Belt came whites to mingle with blacks and drink, dance, see black comedians and dancers, hear black bands playing the new hot music. These clubs with mixed black and white audiences came to be called "black and tans."

One July day Louis Armstrong boarded a train

headed for Chicago, carrying with him only the clothes he was wearing, a few dollars, his cornet, and a fish sandwich made for him by Mayann. He was a classic American figure, the nervous young man striking out on his own for the big city to find fame and fortune. He would, of course, have King Oliver to look after him and introduce him to the ways of the big, cold northern city. Although he knew most of the men in Oliver's Creole Jazz Band, who were mainly from New Orleans, still he would be moving into a strange place filled with strangers.

Louis sat on the train staring nervously out the window at the scenery flashing by. He ate his fish sandwich and some other sandwiches he bought along the way, slept sitting up in his seat, and arrived in Chicago the next evening. The Oliver band had already gone to work, and there was nobody at the station to meet him. He hadn't the least idea where Lincoln Gardens was, or anything else in Chicago, for that matter. But the cab drivers all knew, so Louis took a cab out to the South Side and walked into the dance hall.

It was much fancier than the dance halls he was used to in New Orleans. There was a false ceiling with artificial maple leaves attached to it, and a large mirrored ball that slowly revolved, flashing spots of light on the ceiling, the walls, the dancers' faces.

But in other respects it was not much different from what he was used to. There was the same thick smoke, the same half darkness, the same mass of churning bodies on the dance floor, the same smell of illegal whiskey and beer, and a jazz band playing the music he had grown up with. He went up to the bandstand. As soon as the number was over the musicians crowded around him. They had all been hearing about how well Little Louis was playing, and they were eager to shake his hand and hear him play. Louis found his seat next to Joe Oliver. Oliver stomped off the next tune, Louis put his cornet to his lips, and suddenly he felt at home.

The next day Oliver took Louis to a rooming house where he had arranged for Louis to live. It was a better place than most of the tenements in the South Side, for Louis was not just an ordinary laboring man, but a musician in one of the South Side's best-known jazz bands. What astonished Louis most about it was the fact that he had a bathroom with a bathtub. He had never before lived in a place with a private bathroom, much less a bathtub. It seemed like the height of luxury.

A day or two later Oliver also brought Louis around to a club called the Dreamland Cafe to hear a young woman who was playing piano in the band there. Her name was Lillian Hardin, and she had previously played in Oliver's Creole Jazz Band for a considerable period. Lil, as everybody called her, was different from the men in the Oliver band. They were all New Orleans men who had seen a good deal of the rough life and had played in a lot of tough places. Lil had been raised in Memphis, had studied classical music as a girl, and then had gone on to Fisk University in Nashville, Tennessee, where she had taken special courses in music. She had moved to Chicago about 1916, and had quickly gotten work as a pianist. She began playing in a music store, demonstrating new tunes for customers. A lot of musicians hung around this particular music store. Sometimes Lil jammed with them, and soon she was hired to work in a place called the Pekin Cafe. The Pekin was an after-hours club that opened when the regular cafes closed around two in the morning. It was frequented by musicians and entertainers, both black and white. Lil's mother, who had made her study classical music, hated jazz and the blues, and for a long time Lil didn't dare tell her mother where she was working. But finally her mother found out, and would let Lil continue to work at the Pekin only if one of the members of the band would bring her home after the job.

By the time Louis came to Chicago, Lil had been a professional pianist for several years and had grown quite sophisticated. Oliver was fond of her and had been telling her about his protégé from back home, Little Louis. She was curious about him, but when she met him she was surprised by what she saw. After hearing what a wonderful musician Louis was, she expected a tall man dressed in the finest, most expensive clothes. Instead she found a short young man, wearing a secondhand suit, a gaudy tie, and old-fashioned high-cut shoes that came over his ankles. He looked like a hayseed from the country, not a hot jazz musician.

And in truth, Louis *was* something of a hick. He had never had much schooling. He had gotten most of his education in Perdido Street, surrounded by people who were illiterate, and knew little of the world. The only times he had been outside his hometown were those long trips on the riverboats, and he had spent most of that time on the boats among New Orleans musicians who were not much more sophisticated than he was. He was an inexperienced newcomer.

Not long after Louis's arrival, Lil Hardin rejoined the Oliver band. Quickly she began to see why the musicians thought so much of Louis. And she began to realize that beneath the secondhand suits and the atrocious ties was a shy, soft-spoken young man who always tried to be polite and courteous and never cause trouble for other people. She grew to like him, and they soon became friends.

Lincoln Gardens, where King Oliver's Creole Jazz Band played, was a black dance hall. Most of the other dance halls and cabarets in the Black Belt were the black and tans, ostensibly meant for blacks but actually intended to attract audiences of whites out for a good time. In these black and tans, the races mixed. Sometimes black men even brought white women to these clubs, something that many whites found shocking. Indeed, in many places in the South a black man who tried to date a white woman would have been lynched. "Nice" middle-class whites considered the black and tans low, dangerous places, but, nonetheless, many "nice" middle-class people came to them. Louis would play in many black and tans during his years in Chicago.

Whites even came to Lincoln Gardens. These, however, were mainly musicians trying to learn about this exciting new music that was coming up from New Orleans. A group of white teenagers, including Muggsy Spanier and Bud Freeman, who would go on to become important jazz musicians as adults, used to sneak in regularly. In fact, the interest of white musicians in this New Orleans music was so great that the management of Lincoln Gardens began putting on special "Midnight Rambles" on Wednesday nights for them. The black dancers would leave, tables would be set up on the dance floor, and the rooms would fill up with white musicians who had finished work for the evening. Among them were many of the very top players in Chicago who were working with the best-known bands at the big hotels and cabarets.

The spread of jazz and the blues across the United States was not caused solely by the attraction of the music itself. There were two other factors involved. One was the growing interest of white Americans in black entertainers. Whites had always been curious about the blacks among them. They saw them as somehow "different" from themselves, and they sometimes wondered what went on in those rows of plantation cabins behind the big house, or in those blocks of tenements in Chicago's South Side and New York's Harlem.

During the nineteenth century there grew up a type of theatrical show, the minstrel, catering to this interest in blacks. These shows were put on by white people with their faces covered with burnt cork. They pretended they were black and danced and sang and told jokes the way they imagined blacks did back on the plantations. Of course this picture of happy days on the plantation was nothing like the truth, but these shows were immensely popular with whites.

After the Civil War, when blacks in the South were set free, blacks began to put on minstrel shows of their own in imitation of the white ones. Ironically, these black performers would have to "black up" like whites in order to keep to the traditional minstrel style. Over time, many excellent black performers, especially singers, dancers, and comics, developed. By the turn of the twentieth century some of them, such as the comic song-and-dance team of Bert Williams and George Walker, had become extremely popular.

Through the years that Louis Armstrong was growing up in New Orleans, there was a slow increase in the numbers of blacks in show business. Blacks had been basically responsible for creating the ragtime that was so popular between 1900 and 1920; and many of them, such as the great ragtime composer Scott Joplin, capitalized on it. During the 1910s it became fashionable to have black bands in fancy white restaurants and ballrooms to play for dancing. In fact, the hugely famous dance team of Vernon and Irene Castle danced to a black band led by James Reese Europe.

Then, in 1921, a black show called *Shuffle Along*, written by two black musicians, Eubie Blake and Noble Sissle, became a great hit on Broadway. *Shuffle Along* sparked an interest in black shows, and all through the 1920s more and more black shows were produced. Louis Armstrong would eventually become well known in one. The number of black bands at important hotels and ballrooms increased, and blacks more and more appeared in those brand-new entertainment media: radio and the movies.

For black entertainers the 1920s were boom times, and this made the jazz that the New Orleans blacks were bringing north more acceptable. But there was something else in the air. World War I, which ran from 1914 to 1918, had cost the lives of millions of young men, mainly Europeans, who had died fighting uselessly over small patches of ground. People in both Europe and the United States had been horrified by the needless slaughter, and many were coming to believe that Europe had become decadent and depraved—an old, sick, tired society. New ideas and new ways of doing things would henceforward come from America. American skyscrapers, American superhighways, American jazz, American leisure styles— these would lead the way.

Many young American artists, writers, and intellectuals felt this way. A new American wind was blowing through the world and would make it a fresher place. To these intellectuals, jazz was very much a part of the new spirit. It was more directly emotional than other types of music, they believed; it was lively and fresh. As a matter of fact, many of these intellectuals also believed that blacks themselves were more expressive than whites. It was not just whites who believed this; black intellectuals believed it, too, and they believed that blacks would play an important part in making the fresh, new world that many people saw coming.

These people of the 1920s were, unfortunately, over-optimistic. By the end of the decade the world would be in a financial crisis, and fascism would be growing in Europe. But in the meantime everything worked together to bring jazz forward. It was just the right sort of music to go along with an evening of dancing and drinking in the illegal clubs sprouting up all over the United States.

For black musicians they were flush times, especially in Chicago where the gang-run entertainment industry roared along night after night. The Oliver band was never out of work; when it was not playing at Lincoln Gardens, it toured through the Midwest, playing black dance halls. The names of the musicians in the band were becoming well known, at least to the growing body of jazz fans: Johnny Dodds on clarinet, his brother Baby Dodds on drums (both of whom had been on the riverboats with Armstrong), Honoré Dutrey on trombone, Lil Hardin on piano, Bill Johnson on bass or banjo, and of course Louis Armstrong on second cornet.

People were particularly impressed by the way

Oliver and Armstrong played "breaks" together. A break occurs when the entire band suddenly stops, and one instrument is left alone to improvise freely for a few measures. Oliver and Armstrong had developed a system of playing breaks together, with Louis playing a harmony to Oliver's brief melody. Even musicians were astonished by the trick. Actually, it was not very difficult. Sometime during the song Oliver would play the phrase he intended to use in the next break. Louis would know when the signal was coming, and, being a good musician, would have no difficulty working out a harmony part instantaneously.

Louis was happy in Chicago, happy to be playing in what many people believed was the best jazz band in the United States, happy to be making fifty dollars a week—big pay for anyone in those days, much less a young black man, happy to be free and easy to do what his head told him to do. He was by no means famous. Even the other musicians who came around to the Midnight Rambles at Lincoln Gardens didn't yet realize what a wonderful musician Louis was. The big, domineering Oliver was the star; Louis was merely the second trumpet. Yet for a young man it was glorious enough just being part of the band and playing that music he loved so much every night. What could be better?

But already, when Louis had been with the band for only a few months, some of the other members of the band, and people close to it who knew the members well, were saying quietly that Louis was far better than Joe Oliver, and that he ought to get out from under Oliver's shadow and get a band of his own that he could star in. When people whispered these things to Louis he shook his head emphatically. He was Joe Oliver's boy; he would never upstage the man who had done so much for him.

# CHAPTER EIGHT

In April 1923 King Oliver's Creole Jazz Band went into a recording studio and cut the first in a series of what were to be extremely important jazz records. These were not the first jazz records; those had been made by the Original Dixieland Jazz Band in 1917. Other jazz bands had recorded thereafter, but surprisingly few of them, considering the huge success of the Original Dixieland Jazz Band. However, in 1920 the OKeh Recording Company issued a recording of "Crazy Blues" by a black singer named Mamie Smith. The record astonished even the OKeh executives by becoming a best-seller. A boom in blues records began. Most of the blues records were sold to blacks in the big cities eager to hear the music they remembered from down South; but many whites interested in black entertainment bought them, too.

The blues boom swept up a lot of jazz with it, because jazz bands featured a lot of blues. In 1923 Gennett Records, located in Richmond, Indiana, decided to get in on the blues boom. It was of course a white company, and the owners didn't know much about black bands. They asked around, and somebody told them that King Oliver's band was the best in the North. And so Gennett brought the Oliver band to Richmond to record. After that, through 1923, the band recorded for Columbia, Paramount, OKeh, and again for Gennett. This series of records was the first good sample of New Orleans jazz to be cut. Some indication of how important these records are is given by the fact that all of them are still in print and available in most major cities around the world. Listeners unfamiliar with this early jazz will undoubtedly have difficulty liking the records at first. For one thing, they were acoustic recordings. The musicians gathered around a horn two feet in diameter and four or five feet long. The sound was carried to a needle that vibrated in a revolving plate of wax. A master record was then made from the wax, and from this master copies could be printed. The sound of these records is quite tinny to the modern ear.

For another thing, this New Orleans jazz was ensemble music, with seven or eight instruments going at once, and it is sometimes hard for the ear unfamiliar with it to sort the instruments out. The basic idea was for the cornet to play the melody lead, the clarinet to play filigrees above, or drop through the lead, and the trombone to play figures connecting the phrases of the melody below. The horns were supported by a rhythm section of drums, piano, banjo, and either bass or tuba. In the case of the Creole Jazz Band there was also Louis Armstrong's second cornet, which played a loose harmony to the lead. The sound of all these parts meshing can be very exciting once the ear gets used to it.

Moreover, the music moves along with an easy, rocking swing that gets the feet tapping.

Because Oliver was the dominant figure in the band, Louis doesn't stand out very much in most of these records. He plays a few breaks—including some of the famous double breaks with Oliver, especially on "Snake Rag." But on three of these records Louis stepped forward to play solos of his own. These are "Chimes Blues," "Froggie Moore," and "Riverside Blues," which was issued in two versions. And it is clear from these brief solos that Louis was already well ahead of everybody else in the band—indeed, anywhere—in playing jazz. His tone is full, his attack clean. He plays with more swing than anybody else, and although he is not yet inventing whole long improvising passages, he is beginning to show evidence of the great imaginative powers that marked him as a genius.

But nobody was ready yet to catch on. Louis's name was not mentioned on the records, and listeners had no idea who he was. Only the people in the band, and those who were friends of the musicians in it, realized how fine a jazz player Louis Armstrong really was.

One person who realized it, however, was Lil Hardin. The longer she knew Louis, the more she liked him, and the more she recognized what a great musician he could be. She fell in love with him. They began to go around together, and, finally, on February 5, 1924, they were married.

Lil was proud of her husband and wanted to see him make as much of himself as he could. She made him get rid of the secondhand clothes he had been wearing and took him around to a store where she picked out new ones for him. He was getting overweight, and she put him on a diet. Louis did not like the diet very much, and at meals he would say, "Tweet, tweet," because she was feeding him nothing but "bird seed," he claimed. Most important, she began trying to persuade him to quit the Oliver band and go out on his own.

Louis resisted. He owed a lot to Oliver, and to tell the truth he was somewhat in awe of the older man. Lil grumbled that whenever Joe came to see them, "you'd think that God had walked in." Then, in the spring of 1924 the Creole Jazz Band began to fall apart on its own. The fault was mainly Oliver's. The other musicians were beginning to resent his bossy ways. They also discovered that Oliver was holding out part of their pay: He had been getting more per man from Lincoln Gardens than he had told the musicians and putting the rest in his pocket. When they found out, there was an argument. Honoré Dutrey and the Dodds brothers threatened to beat up Oliver, and they gave notice. The time was now ripe for Louis to leave, and he put in his notice, too.

The question was, What to do next? For the moment he went to work for a bandleader named Ollie Powers at the Dreamland Cafe, where Oliver had first taken him to meet Lil.

Back in New York, however, there was another leader who had Louis Armstrong in mind. This was Fletcher Henderson, the sophisticated black bandleader who had heard Louis in New Orleans while on tour. Henderson was now leader of a big dance orchestra that played arranged music. The Henderson orchestra was growing popular in New York and had been hired to play at the Roseland, New York's most elegant and best-known ballroom, starting in the fall. The Roseland Ballroom, like most dance halls in New York, was segregated for whites only, although of course the band would be black.

We should realize that jazz did not just "come naturally" to blacks. It had been developed by blacks in New Orleans out of other kinds of music, like ragtime and the blues, that had also been developed in the South. The black musicians of the North knew no more about jazz—or the blues as far as that goes—than white musicians did. They were curious about it and interested in it, but they had to learn it just as the whites did.

As a consequence, the musicians in Henderson's band were not very good jazz players. Going into the Roseland was a big opportunity for Henderson, and to make the most of it he knew that he should add at least one really good jazz musician to play solos and special jazz features. He remembered Louis Armstrong. He had heard vaguely that Louis was in Chicago working at the Dreamland. He sent him a wire, offering him a job with his orchestra. He didn't really expect Louis to respond; but Louis, with Lil urging him on, was now ready to accept the challenge. New York was the center of the entertainment business, and there he would be featured as a soloist in one of the city's best-known locations. It was a chance for him to make a name. So he and Lil went East.

In many respects the New York of the time was like Chicago. The gangsters hadn't quite taken over as they had in Chicago, but they were running on a loose rein. There were illegal drinking clubs called "speakeasies" all over the city. Harlem was very much like the Black Belt of Chicago. It was at that time not so run down as the South Side was, and offered a good deal of decent housing for blacks. But in Harlem, too, there were endless cabarets and dance halls run by white gangsters, and special clubs meant to attract white audiences. And of course it meant good times for black entertainers.

Louis joined the Henderson band at rehearsal in a Harlem club called Happy Rhone's. When he walked in and introduced himself, he was very nervous. The Henderson men may not have been in Louis's class as jazz players, but they were all good musicians and quick sight readers. They prided themselves on their expensive clothes and their sophisticated life-style. They were sharps from the big time; and meeting them, Louis felt a little like a hick. He took the third trumpet chair—in dance bands the featured soloist usually played third in order to save his lip for his solos. Then, as they were about to start the first number, the bass player accidentally allowed his instrument to bump against the trombonist's instrument. The trombonist instantly began cursing the bass player. Louis breathed a sigh of relief; these big-time sharps were regular people, too.

Nonetheless, Louis felt somewhat out of place among the sophisticated and assertive New York musicians in the Henderson band. These men believed that the band was the best black dance band in New York and probably the whole United States, and they were cocky and sure of themselves. Louis felt somewhat uneasy about blowing the kind of hot jazz solos he could play.

Then something happened to change that. Henderson was looking for a good clarinetist who could read music and also play jazz solos. He asked Louis if he knew anybody. Louis remembered a Memphis musician named Buster Bailey, who had been playing around Chicago. He told Henderson about Bailey, and Henderson sent for him. Bailey was happy to have the opportunity to play with the Henderson band and quickly came to New York. At the first rehearsal Henderson called for a fast jazz number, "Tiger Rag," to test Bailey out. The band roared into the tune, and when Bailey's turn came he blew one hot chorus after another. Suddenly Louis felt challenged. When it came his turn, he shot into his solo like a skyrocket. Exploding chorus after chorus, he filled the air with showers of golden notes, so audacious that the other musicians were stunned. When he was finished there was no doubt in anybody's mind who the king of jazz was, and from then on Louis got over his shyness and was able to play with the fire and strength he knew he had.

It is paradoxical that however shy he was personally, once Louis Armstrong got up on the bandstand he was an entirely different person, confident and unafraid.

At the Roseland Ballroom, the Henderson band was a success right from the start. The dancers loved their music, and their reputation started to grow. Musicians began to come around to hear them; even black musicians were permitted to come in the back way and stand out of sight to listen. Soon a radio company began to broadcast the band from Roseland for a half hour or so several evenings a week. The band was becoming famous.

The general public didn't single out Louis for special appreciation. As far as they were concerned he was just another member of the band. But the musicians who crowded around knew better. They could feel that intense swing Louis put into his playing, and they were excited by the constant stream of new musical phrases he seemed to be able to spin off so easily. They were deeply impressed by him. Some, in fact, were flatly awed. Rex Stewart, a young black trumpeter who would become an important jazz soloist himself, was so enamored of Louis's playing that he began to dress like Louis, walk like Louis, hang around outside Louis's apartment building just to catch a glimpse of him. Others did not go as far as Stewart, but they all wanted to discover the secret of his playing, and they studied him carefully.

The men in the Henderson band heard him play one brilliant solo after another every night. Gradually they began to capture some of the feeling of swing that Louis put into his playing. And over that winter of 1924 and 1925, the Fletcher Henderson band changed. It was becoming a hard-swinging jazz band. Armstrong alone did not change the band. Jazz was the exciting new thing and was in the air everywhere. The musicians in the Henderson band, and in New York in general, were hearing records by Bix Beiderbecke, Jelly Roll Morton, the Original Dixieland Jazz Band, and the Memphis Five, who had caught on to the new music earlier. But because Armstrong was sitting among them, he was the major figure in teaching them how jazz should be played. Some of them, such as saxophonist Coleman Hawkins, caught on quickly and started their own development as important jazz musicians.

As the popularity of the Henderson band soared, record companies began asking them to record. At that time few bands had exclusive contracts with a single company but could record for any of them, even doing the same number several times for different labels. During this period the Henderson band was in the studios regularly, once or twice a month. Louis played solos on almost half of these sides. They are the first really good examples of his jazz playing we have, and they make clear just how far ahead of everybody else he was. For example, on a very corny record called "Go 'long Mule," the band thumps and bumps along very much like a mule until Louis comes tearing in, ripping off a blazing hot solo that leaves the rest of the band gasping in the dust. Louis also played wonderful solos on such Henderson records as "Copenhagen," "Shanghai Shuffle," "How Come You Do Me Like You Do?" and many others. However, his most famous record with Henderson was "Sugarfoot Stomp." This was actually a tune originally called "Dippermouth Blues" and was a special feature number worked out by King Oliver to show off his skill with the plunger, or "wa-wa," mute. Oliver had cut the tune twice with the Creole Jazz Band while Louis was in it, and the records were justly admired by musicians. When Louis came to New York to join the Henderson band, the arranger asked him if there were any number he wanted for a feature. He chose this tune. On the record he does not use the "wa-wa" plunger mute as Oliver had, but the smoother straight mute, and he plays three moving choruses of blues on it. The record was a hit for Henderson and remained in print for ten years.

During this period Fletcher Henderson was frequently asked to put together little informal backup groups for blues singers. He usually chose men from his own orchestra for these groups. Louis, of course, had grown up with the blues, and he was on most of these, backing some of the most famous blues singers of the day. Particularly admired are a set of five he made with Bessie Smith, widely regarded as the finest blues singer of all time. The version of the classic tune "St. Louis Blues" that these two giants made together remains one of the greatest of all blues recordings.

Louis was also being recorded by another bandleader named Clarence Williams, a piano player from New Orleans. Williams frequently brought into the studios the New Orleans musicians he found around New York and recorded them playing New Orleans-style jazz under such names as the Clarence Williams Blue Five and the Red Onion Jazz Babies. He teamed Armstrong on some of these records with Sidney Bechet, a clarinetist and soprano saxophonist from New Orleans, who was only a step behind Louis in his jazz feeling. Together they made some superb records, including a scorching hot "Cake-Walking Babies from Home" and a slow, twisting blues called "Texas Moaner Blues," which is one of the best samples we have of how the blues were played in the honky-tonks of New Orleans.

These records, taken together, show Louis Armstrong developing a new aspect to his style. That was a sense of what we can call "architecture." By this we mean the ability to give his improvised melodies a shape that was novel and interesting, but at the same time made sense. In "Go 'long Mule" he divided the first six measures into three parallel figures. Each of these opens with three quarter notes (a beat long) followed by a patch of quicker notes, so that he seems to be having a conversation with himself. In his "Copenhagen" he shapes figures that are variations on ones that came before. In this solo we can also see how he constantly reverses direction, going up and down, down and up, where a less gifted player might continue on straight up or down.

Yet one other facet of Armstrong's music began to come out during this stay with Henderson. Louis had always liked to sing, going all the way back to the time when he was eight years old and singing for pennies on the street corners of New Orleans. He still sang whenever he got the chance, although he had not had much opportunity to do so with the Oliver band.

In New York he began badgering Fletcher Henderson to let him sing. Henderson was reluctant. Louis had a rough, raspy voice, which Henderson thought sounded like a "fish horn." Nonetheless, he allowed Louis to try singing a few comical numbers, especially "How Come You Do Me Like You Do?" It made a hit with audiences. Despite the coarseness of his voice, Louis was a natural musician and could sing in tune, with a lot of swing. So Henderson let Louis sing an occasional number at the Roseland. But he never allowed Louis to sing on records.

This upset Louis. He recognized that it was far easier to get a name by singing than simply by being the featured jazz soloist in a band. If audiences liked his singing, why not let him record? But Henderson was adamant.

Louis might have accepted this, but he was already becoming disenchanted with the Henderson band. Many of the men were heavy drinkers, and as a whole the band was often lax about its music, not showing up on the bandstand on time, and often being casual about the way they played. Louis was serious about his music, and didn't like this too-relaxed attitude.

There were other points, too. Henderson had

brought another trumpet soloist, named Joe Smith, into the band. Smith was a fine player, but he was not up to Louis as a jazz player, and Louis resented Henderson's giving Smith a lot of solos. Furthermore, his wife Lil had gone back to Chicago to be with her mother, who was ill. She wanted Louis to come home.

Finally, in September of 1925, when Louis had been with Henderson for a year, Lil wired him that she had arranged a job for him to lead a band under his own name at the fancy Dreamland, at a salary of seventy-five dollars a week, a large sum at that time for a relatively unknown musician. The time was ripe. So late in October he headed back to Chicago. It was a fateful move, for he had hardly been there for two weeks when he went into the OKeh recording studios to cut the first of what would be one of the most important series of records ever made in the United States.

# CHAPTER NINE

Louis Armstrong came back to Chicago far better known than when he left. He was still not a name to the general public, even the black public. But musicians knew about him, and so did the small but growing group of jazz fans, both black and white, who were following the music and studying it as best they could. The black newspaper, the *Chicago Defender*, which circulated all around the United States, announced his return in a special story:

> Mr. Armstrong, the famous cornetist, will grace the first chair in the Dreamland Orchestra sometime this week. Williams Bottoms has made him an unusual salary offer to return to Chicago. Mr. Armstrong has been the feature cornetist with the Famous Fletcher Henderson orchestra. . . .

The Dreamland was typical of the cabarets, or nightclubs, as they were later called, that Louis Armstrong was to play in for the next fifteen years. The cabaret as an institution had been developed after 1910 as a combination dance hall, restaurant, and theater. The typical cabaret was in a large room with tables spread around the floor. At one end would be a bandstand, with a small space in front of it for dancing. The customers would sit at their tables, drink, eat, listen to the music, and from time to time get up and dance.

Two or three times each evening the dance floor would be cleared, and a show, sometimes quite elaborate, would be put on. It would usually include a comedian or two, a dancer or dance team, a singer, perhaps a comic skit or playlet, and a feature or two from the orchestra.

Some of these clubs were quite elegant. The Dreamland had a solid glass dance floor and little lights set low on the wall to illuminate the dancers' feet. However elegant they were, in most big cities they were controlled by gangsters and frequented by many tough people. Sometimes the gangsters who owned them would lock the doors and hold private parties for themselves. In some cases a gangster would give the bandleader a tip of several hundred dollars and order him to play the gangster's favorite song over and over all night. Other times gang members pulled out guns and shot the place up just for fun, perhaps blasting away at the bass while the musicians dove for cover.

Over the next four years, from the fall of 1925 until the spring of 1929, Louis played in a number of such cabarets around Chicago. There were of course whites-only cabarets in Chicago, but the ones Louis played in mostly were located on the South Side, and were racially mixed black and tans. The music he played in these cabarets was much the same as what the Henderson band had played—dance music with a good deal of jazz mixed in.

During most of this period Louis also played at black theaters. That was the day of silent movies. In order to make them more dramatic, most theaters had some sort of music to accompany the film—suspenseful music when the hero was dangling from a window ledge, happy music when the boy and girl got together at the end. In small theaters the music might be provided by a piano; but in big-city theaters, like the ones that Louis played in, there would be quite elaborate arrangements for a whole orchestra to accompany the film.

These theaters usually presented some kind of show as well as a movie. There might be a comedian, a singer, a dancer. Usually the orchestra would be featured as well. Louis played in the Erskine Tate orchestra, one of the most famous of these theater bands. It usually played a symphonic overture, as well as a jazz feature.

The places Louis was playing in now were somewhat different from where he had played before. In the tonks of black Storyville, on the riverboats, at the Lincoln Gardens, at the Roseland Ballroom with the Henderson band, he had been playing music for dancing. Now, in the theaters and cabarets of Chicago, dance music was only a part of what was needed. The bands had to back singers and dancers and play special features. The stars were not so much the soloists in the orchestras, but the singers, dancers, and comics who stepped out front and put on their own acts.

Louis saw this, and he was beginning to feel that

just being a cornet player was not enough. He had always loved singing, and he had always had a comical way about him—he was "jokified," as the boys at the Waifs' Home had said. Perhaps he could step out front a little bit, too.

To do so, however, he would have to overcome his shyness. It was one thing to sit in the ranks of a band, even playing solos; it was quite another to step out in front of the band and sing, dance, tell jokes. He wanted to do it, all right; he wanted to get all these people out there cheering and applauding him. But he was having trouble getting up the nerve. Once Erskine Tate heard Louis warming up on a pretty tune of the time, called "Little Stars of Duna, Carry Me Home." He told Louis he'd pay him twenty-five dollars extra to play the number as a solo, but Louis was too shy, and he turned the offer down.

Yet he knew he had to get over his shyness, and it finally happened after he started working at a cabaret called the Sunset Cafe, with a band led by a man named Carroll Dickerson. The star singer at the Sunset was a pretty young woman named Mae Alix. Somebody had written a comic specialty number for her called "Big Butter and Egg Man from Out West." It called for a male singer, too, somebody who could get some laughs out of the lyric and do a few simple dance steps. Louis, it occurred to some of the people in charge of the show, was a natural to do the song with Mae.

Louis resisted; it meant getting out on the floor in

front of the band. But the people in charge virtually ordered him to do it, at the risk of losing his job. There was no way out of it, so Louis rehearsed the song with Mae Alix and a few nights later stepped out into the spotlight with her and sang and danced. By the time he finished he was sweating with embarrassment, but the audience loved the performance. They roared with laughter and cheered. From then on Louis was called out front every night to sing "Big Butter and Egg Man from Out West."

Gradually he got over his nervousness. He began throwing little comic touches into his songs, changing the lyrics here and there to make them funnier and playing with the melody a little as he did on the cornet. Sometimes he would "scat" parts of the song—that is, sing nonsense syllables instead of the written words.

Once he got used to performing in the spotlight out in front of the band, he began to expand his act. For the theaters he developed a routine in which he would "preach" a comic sermon and finish up with some jazz on his cornet, a routine he interjected into some of his records years later. He had another routine he did with his old friend Zutty Singleton. Zutty had gone into the Navy at the time of World War I and had been late getting in on the jazz boom. By 1926 he was in Chicago, and he and Louis had resumed their old friendship. Louis helped Zutty get a job with the Carroll Dickerson band at the Sunset Cafe, and here they worked out a comic routine in which Zutty, who was a big man, would dress up as a woman, and Louis would play "her" henpecked husband. It was an ancient routine, but audiences roared at it.

Louis, thus, was no longer simply a jazz cornetist, but an all-around entertainer who could play, sing, tell jokes, and even dance a little. In truth, although Louis Armstrong was one of the greatest jazz musicians who ever lived, he was never one exclusively. He had played old favorites with the Waifs' Home band, marches and hymns with the parade bands, dance music on the riverboats and at the Roseland. He always played jazz, too; but he prided himself on being a competent professional musician who could play anything that was called for. It came naturally to him to clown and jive with his audiences.

He by no means forgot how to play jazz, however. In November 1925, he went into the OKeh studios to make the first of the crucial set of records that are generally known as the Hot Five series. From the moment Louis returned to Chicago it was clear, to people in the music business at least, that he ought to record under his own name. Nobody was really sure whether his records would sell, but there was a feeling that it would be worth trying. Moreover, Lil was eager to see him rise up. If he was to be anybody in music, he had to have his own recording group.

Probably the man most responsible for getting the Hot Five series started was Richard Myknee (pronounced My-nee) Jones. Like Clarence Williams, who had recorded Louis in New York, Myknee Jones was a black New Orleanian pianist who had come north in the black wave and had become an entrepreneur—somebody who got things done. Jones was a talent scout for OKeh, and it was probably he who suggested that the company record Louis. He then got together with Lil, who was actually managing Louis, and they worked up a band. Lil would play piano, but the rest of the musicians would be New Orleanians. Johnny Dodds, who had worked with Louis on the riverboats and again with Oliver, would play clarinet. The trombonist would be Kid Ory, who had left California and was in Chicago working with the King Oliver band. On banjo there would be Johnny St. Cyr, a highly regarded musician from the old hometown. On November 12, 1925, the five musicians went into the OKeh studios to cut the first of the Hot Five records.

Recording techniques were in a rapid state of advancement. Most important, the old acoustical system was being phased out in favor of the electrical system, still being developed. The new system used a gadget called a microphone in place of the old, cumbersome horn. One great advantage of the microphone was that it picked up sound better from distances than the old horn had, so the musicians did not need to be grouped next to it, but could sit or stand around it in a more normal fashion. Furthermore, the old system had no volume control, either in recording or in playing back. In the electrical system engineers could raise and lower the volume level as necessary. Over the next few years the electrical system would be improved almost on a daily basis and would take over entirely by the end of the 1920s. (Actually, the first Hot Five session was recorded acoustically; but all the rest, electrically.)

Nonetheless, recording was still very primitive by modern standards. For one thing, neither OKeh nor many other companies had studios outside their home cities. They used traveling studios, which were set up in warehouses, offices, even people's living rooms. The records were cut into a great wheel of wax, and, if something went wrong, the top layer of wax was scraped off and thrown away and they tried again on the fresh surface.

Engineers had a lot of trouble making turntables revolve at steady speeds. As a consequence, many of these early records play either too fast or too slow. Most of them have been reissued uncorrected, so that today we still hear many early jazz classics at the wrong speed. But despite the defects, the sound on these Hot Fives is not at all bad—far easier listening than the sides Louis had made with Oliver only two years earlier.

When we consider the enormous care, expense and hundreds of hours that go into making modern records, we are astonished at how casually these jazz masterpieces were tossed off. When OKeh was about to bring its recording equipment to Chicago, Myknee Jones or somebody else would call Louis or Lil and say that they should have so many tunes ready. Usually they would cut six or eight sides over two or three days.

(These were 78 rpm records that lasted about three minutes a side.) Louis or Lil or somebody else in the band would work out a few sketchy tunes. They might have a brief rehearsal in Louis's living room, but sometimes they simply ran through the tune once in the recording studio and then cut it. Usually there would be two or three takes of each side to get one right. They would cut two to four records over six to eight hours, collect fifty dollars each, and that would be that. To these musicians, records were strictly a side matter to the important work of playing in theaters and cabarets—a way to earn a few extra dollars and gain a little ego satisfaction, but nothing else.

In the fall of 1925, when the first of the Hot Fives were cut, most of the musicians in the group were working primarily in dance and show bands in clubs and theaters, playing arrangements they read or had memorized. The first of the Hot Fives, however, were in the old New Orleans style that these people knew so well. Louis was somewhat nervous to be cutting records under his own leadership. With Oliver and Henderson he had been a "side man," to use the musicians' term, and had only his own part to worry about. As leader he had to set tempos and, in general, carry more of the responsibility. He also had to play the cornet lead around which the other musicians spun their lines. At that first Hot Five recording session he was nervous. But the session went well, and the records sold well enough that OKeh asked Armstrong to cut some more sides. This time Myknee Jones suggested that Louis sing on a couple of the records. His first recorded vocal was on a tune called "Georgia Grind." It was a poor tune, and Louis's singing was only passable. But immediately afterward the band cut a comic novelty tune called "Heebie Jeebies" that Louis also sang. It was not a great tune either, but Louis made something special out of it by scatting the lyrics.

It has usually been said that the scat vocal on "Heebie Jeebies" came about by accident. Louis, so the story goes, dropped the sheet of paper with the words and started scatting instead. Myknee Jones remembers Louis grabbing the microphone and pulling it down with him as he bent over to pick up the paper, scatting all the time. Jones bent over, too, to pick up the paper, and they bumped heads.

The story may be true, and it may not. In any case, "Heebie Jeebies" made a hit with the public, especially blacks on Chicago's South Side. It sold forty thousand copies in a few weeks, a big sale for the time.

The success of "Heebie Jeebies" made it clear to everybody that Louis, despite his funny, rough voice, had a future as a singer. From that moment on Myknee Jones and the other executives at OKeh had Louis sing more and more frequently, until within a few months he was singing on almost every record he cut. Fletcher Henderson, clearly, had made a mistake in not letting Louis sing with his orchestra. With each record from the Hot Five, Louis's popularity increased. OKeh began to advertise the Hot Five records in the black newspaper, the *Chicago Defender*, and that, too, helped to spread Louis's name.

At first his fans were mainly black people living in big-city slums, many of them fresh from the South. But white musicians, who already knew about Armstrong from his two years with King Oliver's Creole Jazz Band and his records with Fletcher Henderson, very quickly began buying Hot Five records and playing them until they were scratchy and worn. The musicians were more and more impressed by Louis's mastery of his horn and his wonderful improvisations. They made their friends listen to the Hot Five records, and soon the growing number of serious jazz fans all over the United States came to realize that Louis Armstrong was somebody special.

Although the musicians and the serious jazz fans enjoyed Louis's singing, it was his cornet playing that drew them to the records. They were entranced by the swing that he got into everything he played, by his great technical skill, and by his brilliant melodic inventions.

We can hardly discuss here all of the great records in the Hot Five series. Perhaps the most famous are "Cornet Chop Suey," "Potato Head Blues," "Big Butter and Egg Man," "Tight Like This," and "West End Blues," as well as his first hit, "Heebie Jeebies." Every jazz fan would have his own special favorites to add to the list.

What is most important to notice is Louis's musical growth over the three years in which this series was cut. The first of these records are in the happy-go-lucky spirit of good times remembered from New Orleans. They are full of good cheer. Furthermore, in his solos Louis tends to paraphrase the melody of the song. That is to say, suggestions of the original melody keep cropping up in his solo line.

As the series progresses, we can see steady growth. Not only does Louis depart more and more from the sometimes simple melodies of the songs to make wholly new and startling melodies, but there is also an emotional deepening in his playing. No longer is he content to dance along, handing out good cheer. Now he has other, more complex things to say, more painful things to express. He is saying that life is not always pleasant, that bad things, even tragic things, happen to people. Such songs as "Tight Like This" and "Potato Head Blues," despite their comic titles, are filled with sorrow.

This new, deeper approach to his music was undoubtedly in part due to a tragedy in Louis's life. During his years in Chicago he frequently invited his mother, Mayann, to visit him and Lil in the new home Lil had bought for them, which had plenty of extra room. Louis was by now supporting Mayann, in any case. On one of those visits, in 1927, Mayann became ill. Louis and Lil cared for her and worried over her, but it was no use, and she died. Mayann had not been a perfect mother to Louis, but nonetheless she had always loved him and always allowed him to go his own way. When Mayann died Louis didn't make much

**B**y the end of 1928 when he made the last of the Hot Five records, Louis Armstrong was recognized as being in a class by himself as a jazz musician. There were other fine musicians around, especially the white cornetist Bix Beiderbecke, whom many people, including Louis, admired. But Louis was special; the musicians worshipped him, and the growing number of serious jazz fans idolized him. Bunny Berigan, a very fine jazz musician himself, once said, "The first thing a musician packs when he goes on the road is a picture of Louis Armstrong." Louis had come a long way from that tambourine in the Waifs' Home band.

This idolization of Louis had profound effects on jazz. At the time that Louis was first recording with Henderson and his own Hot Five in the mid-1920s, people had a lot of different ideas about what jazz was and how it should be played. Some thought it ought to be written out in careful arrangements; others thought it ought to be played in the rough New Orleans style of the Oliver band; still others believed it should combine both styles, or take things from classical music.

But when musicians discovered Louis Armstrong, almost overnight they decided that this was the way jazz should be played. They reached this conclusion not by thinking it through logically, but simply because Louis's music excited them so: If it felt so good to hear that music, what must it be like to play it? So they began taking things from Louis's style. They tried, for one thing, to capture the swing he got in his playing. For another, they saw from his work what marvelous things could be done with improvising.

Finally, as the Hot Five series progressed, the producers at OKeh realized that Louis was the selling point for the records, and they kept bringing him more and more to the forefront. The first of the Hot Fives were in the New Orleans style, with more ensemble playing than solos. Indeed, on many of these records the clarinetist, Johnny Dodds, soloed more often than Louis, as he had done on the Oliver Creole Jazz Band records. But step by step the ensembles were curtailed to give Louis more room to play and sing. And by the time the last of these records were made, they consisted of strings of solos, with just enough ensemble to maintain a little of the old spirit. In so doing, Louis had turned jazz from a music of worked-out ensembles into one in which the main point was the improvised solo. It has been this ever since.

During the Hot Five period Louis switched from cornet to trumpet. The instruments are very much the same, except that the cornet is designed to have a somewhat softer, mellower tone than the more brilliant trumpet. Louis made the change in part to match his sound to the other trumpet players in the theater orchestras he played in. But basically he made the switch because he decided he liked the sound of the trumpet better than the cornet. We do not know exactly when he changed, but it was probably gradually through 1927.

It was not just musicians, but the general black public, too, who were becoming increasingly aware of Louis. They of course enjoyed his music, but there was more to it than that. In the United States it was widely believed that blacks were basically inferior to whites. They were not as smart as whites, people said, nor as artistic, nor as energetic. Blacks were lazy, so the idea went, and there were certain kinds of things you could not expect blacks to be able to do, such as write great symphonies, or become great actors or national leaders.

Not all whites believed these things, but most of them did. Unhappily, so did a lot of blacks, even if they didn't often admit it to anybody, or even to themselves. When they looked around they saw few black college professors, few black Shakespearean actors, few black novelists and poets. Whites were better at almost everything than blacks were, so it seemed. There might be a few exceptions, of course, but what was there to indicate that blacks as a group were as clever and talented as whites?

By the beginning of 1929, however, it was clear to blacks that Louis Armstrong was not merely a great jazz musician: He was the *best*. Even white people admitted that white musicians looked up to Louis and attempted to imitate him. To blacks, who were often discouraged about themselves, it meant a great deal that here at least was one black man who was better than whites at what he did.

Louis was not the only black who was clearly superior to whites at what he did. A few years before a black boxer named Jack Johnson had shocked the white world by beating the white champion and becoming World Heavyweight Champion. There were excellent black writers, painters, and actors coming along, too, like Paul Robeson and Richard Wright. But nobody was saying that Robeson and Wright were *the* best; and Jack Johnson had long since been defeated. But about Louis there was no argument; he was the best, and blacks took a great deal of pride in this fact. In 1929 Louis made a visit to New York, where he was given a dinner by white musicians. This was unusual in itself at the time, but they also gave Louis a watch inscribed "To the World's Greatest Trumpet Player," and that was even more unusual. The *Chicago Defender* made a point of covering the story for its black readers.

But if jazz musicians, fans, and many ordinary black people knew and admired Louis Armstrong, he still had not made much of a name with the general American public, which was of course about ninety percent white. Now circumstances were about to change all that.

In 1928 there was an election in Chicago that brought in a reform government. The new people clamped down on the criminals who had been doing as they liked in the city, and closed down a lot of the illegal bars and clubs the racketeers owned. This was all to the good, generally; but it hurt the musicians. With the cabarets closing down, scores of musicians were thrown out of work. Suddenly there were bad times in Chicago.

Not long before OKeh had brought in a new record producer to replace Myknee Jones. This was a white, Tommy Rockwell, a tough, hard drinking, hard-cursing Texan, who nonetheless was a good salesman and was an excellent judge of what the public liked. Rockwell was producer for the Hot Five records from the spring of 1927. Naturally he and Louis got to know each other quite well, and at some point, probably late in 1928, Louis signed with Rockwell to manage him.

It was not necessarily the wisest thing for Louis to do. Rockwell was not a criminal or a gangster, but like a lot of people in the entertainment business, he was out for himself and would take advantage of performers when he got a chance. It is a sad truth that the music business in the United States has frequently been infected by people from the underworld. Performers are often cheated of large amounts of money, are talked into signing foolish contracts that give their managers and record companies far too large a share of the profits, are paid off in drugs, which keeps them from paying enough attention to the business part of music.

This was as true in Louis Armstrong's time as it is

today. It was particularly bad for black show people because they were completely closed out of the business side of the entertainment industry. Blacks could not become record producers (except at one or two small, black-owned record companies); they could not manage theaters or dance halls. All of the executive positions in the industry were held by whites.

Louis knew this, and he knew that the only way he could rise in show business was through the intercession of whites. Specifically, he needed a white manager, because show business bosses would have nothing to do with any black manager. Myknee Jones or Clarence Williams might act as black talent scouts, but they could not become executives in theaters and record companies.

So Louis signed with Rockwell. Rockwell was just the sort of tough, hardboiled man, like Benny Williams or King Oliver, that Louis had always been attracted to. He admired tough men and knew they could be helpful to him: A man like Tommy Rockwell could act like a blocking back for Louis. He could open doors that would otherwise remain closed to him.

Thus, even though Tom Rockwell was not reliable about money, he was not a bad choice for Louis. He knew the record business, and he would push his client aggressively.

By the beginning of 1929 Rockwell saw that the entertainment business was in a bad way in Chicago. It was time for Louis to move to New York, the center of show business. He booked Louis into a new New

York club, the Savoy, early in 1929 for a one-night engagement. He was a smash hit, so Rockwell arranged other work for him, and in May Louis set out to live in New York permanently.

He didn't go alone, however. He took with him the whole band he had been working with around Chicago. They were glad to go; times were hard in Chicago, and without Louis they would be just one more band around the city. Louis shouldn't have taken the whole band, for there really was no work for them in New York. But he had some loyalty to them. Moreover, traces of his old shyness remained, and he felt more comfortable challenging this big city again surrounded by people he knew. One of them was his old pal from New Orleans, Zutty Singleton, who played drums in the band.

Tommy Rockwell was nonplussed to see the whole band turn up. He scrambled around and finally found a job for them working in a Harlem cabaret. As had been the case in Chicago, a lot of white people liked going into black neighborhoods for good times. To cater to them, several cabarets had been started in Harlem in the 1920s. Most of these were run by white gangsters. Some of them were black and tans intended for racial mixing, but the most important of them were segregated, where the performers and waiters were blacks, but only whites could sit at the tables.

One of the best known of these Harlem cabarets was Connie's Inn. Like the Chicago cabarets, Connie's Inn put on elaborate shows with dancers, comedians, chorus lines of pretty girls, and even little skits. The show that was running at Connie's Inn when Louis came to town was called *Hot Chocolates*. The music for it had been written by a young black pianist who would become one of the best-known entertainers of his time, and one of the best of all American songwriters, Fats Waller.

*Hot Chocolates* drew huge crowds to Connie's Inn every night, and they left laughing and whistling the songs from the show. It occurred to the people who owned the club that with a little dressing up the show might become a Broadway hit. In 1929 the boom in black entertainment was stronger than ever, with new shows using black casts appearing all the time.

So in June *Hot Chocolates* was moved to Broadway. Connie's Inn now needed a band, and the Armstrong group was hired. But Louis himself was chosen to go into the Broadway show. His part would be small: He would sing one of the big songs from the show, "Ain't Misbehavin'." He would not sing it during the show, but only during intermission, and he would not sing it from the stage, but in the pit in front of the stage where the band sat. The role could hardly have been smaller, but the consequences were large. On opening night, the producers of the show were startled when the crowd roared its approval of Louis's brief performance. They were even more startled the next day when the reviewer for the *New York Times* called Louis's rendition of "Ain't Misbehavin' " one of the high spots of the show. Something in Louis's rough voice touched these sophisticated New York theatergoers. When it became clear that the incident was no accident, but that people loved Louis's singing, the producers brought Louis out of the orchestra pit and onto the stage to do the number. The applause continued, and through the run of the show, Louis's role was enlarged, and enlarged again.

Louis had something that audiences liked; that was clear. It didn't matter that his voice was untrained. There was that infectious swing, there was that great musical talent, and there was something in Louis's manner that struck home. He was, it seemed, warm, honestly eager to please. It was an important quality, and hardly surprising. Growing up as a boy who had nothing and had to depend so frequently on the kindness of other people, how could he not be eager to please?

The shrewd Tommy Rockwell had been right about Louis Armstrong. He was not only a great jazz musician, but he also had that ability to reach out to other people, to touch them, that every popular show business star has. Audiences felt that he was talking to them directly from his heart.

Rockwell immediately set about capitalizing on the small but growing fame that Louis was earning in *Hot Chocolates*. In July, when the show had only been running for four weeks, Rockwell brought him into the OKeh studios to record some of the songs from it, including the tune that he was rapidly making his own, "Ain't Misbehavin'." By this time Louis was singing and playing—and even dancing—in *Hot Chocolates*. He was also racing up to Harlem after his last number in the show to perform at Connie's Inn. And if this were not enough, Tommy Rockwell booked him into a black theater in Harlem for a week. Between times there were more record dates. That whole summer Louis was constantly leaping into cabs and dashing from one date to the next. Sometimes he was so tired that he dozed off in the cab and had to be awakened by the driver at his stop.

This heavy activity was doing more than just tiring Louis out. The punishment he always gave his lip, due to his poor training, was now doubled. It was painful for him just to place the mouthpiece on the flesh, much less bear down on it as he did when he went into the upper register.

And he was playing in the upper register a lot. He had discovered that audiences liked to hear him reach out into the skies for the top notes, and he had started climbing into the upper reaches of the horn at the close of virtually every number. Sometimes he would hit dozens of high Cs one after another at the end of a number and then finish off with an F above high C. It thrilled audiences; but it was destroying his lip.

To compensate, Louis very quickly changed his style. Where he had always been a very busy player, inventing rich, thick, melodic lines with a lot of quick notes in them, he now developed a much simpler, more spare style that used fewer quick notes and left more open space. It was not a worse style; in some ways it was more subtle and better thought-out than his older way of playing. But it was different.

Although the change of style helped some, Louis was still punishing his lip to an extraordinary degree. Sometimes the flesh actually split, spewing blood down his shirt front. Louis would then be forced to stop playing and get by on his singing for a few weeks. Gradually, inevitably, scar tissue built up on his tender flesh.

Unfortunately, Tommy Rockwell neither knew nor cared. He had found himself a star he could rise with. So he booked Louis wherever he could, regardless of the consequences. There was more to come. During this summer, when Louis was becoming a star, he continued to use the band that had come to New York with him from Chicago. He had played with many of these men for several years, and with one of them, Zutty Singleton, for over ten years. They had backed him at Connie's Inn, on records, and at other places he played. But suddenly that fall Tommy Rockwell decided to get rid of them.

His reason was simple: money. Rockwell was also booking a band led by another New Orleanian black, Luis Russell. Rockwell reasoned that he could use the Luis Russell band to back Louis when necessary, thus saving the salaries of the Chicago group. So he told Louis he wanted to fire the band.

Louis was troubled. The Chicago men were counting on Louis to keep them working, and Louis knew it wasn't right just to dump them. But Rockwell talked fast: Louis could be a star, he could be rich, but he would have to follow Rockwell's instruction. He couldn't expect to climb if he had to carry his old band with him. Louis stalled, trying to find some way out of it. But he could not. His hand was finally forced when his old friend Zutty came to see Louis in the hotel where he was living with Lil. Bluntly, Zutty asked Louis what he intended to do about the band.

Louis was embarrassed. He hated to hurt his old friend from New Orleans. But now there was no way around it. He told Zutty what Rockwell had said, that he could be a star and make a lot of money if he did what Rockwell wanted him to do.

"Well, Louie," Zutty said, "I guess friendship is friendship, and business is business, isn't it?" And he left the hotel feeling bitter and resentful toward Louis. He never got over his feeling, and although he and Louis became friendly again, Zutty always carried that moment in his heart.

In fact, Louis didn't have to follow Tommy Rockwell's instructions as slavishly as he did. He was the star, not Rockwell. Rockwell needed Louis far more than Louis needed Rockwell. There were plenty of people around who could provide Louis with good management, and very few performers of Louis's potential. But Louis lacked confidence in himself. He didn't feel that he could stand up to Rockwell, to argue with him, to tell him flatly no, that he would not fire the Chicago men. And he allowed Rockwell to boss him around.

Louis Armstrong was not unique in this; many black performers of the time behaved the same way. Cut off from the management end of show business, they didn't know how things worked—who really had power, and who was just talk. And they often allowed themselves to be talked into doing things they didn't want to do.

In any case, the Chicago band was fired. Zutty got a job playing at Connie's Inn and went on to be a famous jazz musician for three decades. But most of the other men were not so lucky. They crept back to Chicago, and none of them ever played an important role in popular music again.

But for Louis, a line had been crossed: He would become a star.

Over the years between the summer of 1929, when he went into *Hot Chocolates*, and the summer of 1932, when he made an extended trip to Europe, Louis Armstrong became a star. He was leader of his own band, which was on tour almost constantly, playing theaters, dance halls, and nightclubs all across the United States. His band broadcast regularly over the radio. He appeared in his first movies. He was no longer a jazz musician with a small following of devoted fans, but a show business personality, whom the general public knew about and liked.

He was making what for a black man of the time was a substantial income, too. Louis never cared much about having a lot of money. What mattered to him was playing music, and if there was enough money to cover his expenses, he was content. But with his growing popularity his manager was able to demand higher prices for him and his band, and Louis was able to afford things, like new cars and expensive clothes, that he had never had before. The man who only ten years before had seen his first private bathroom was now able to afford luxuries.

But being a star turned out to be not quite so wonderful as it sounded. For one thing, it meant that he had to work almost constantly. His manager wanted him to work as much as possible. Louis could have insisted on taking more time off, but he found it difficult to say no to a white man, especially a tough one like Tommy Rockwell. Moreover, he liked to play. He liked to make music, and he liked to hear those hundreds or thousands of people out there cheering for him.

At times the band "sat down" at a club or a theater for a week or so, but most of the time it played one-nighters, or "split weeks" of three or four days at theaters. The one-nighters were almost always dances, often at run-down dance halls. Sometimes the band would tour through the South, where they would play in ancient halls, or even tobacco barns converted for the evening. Even though the dances were for blacks, they were generally promoted by whites, who at times would try to cheat the band out of its share of the money. There were many other problems with these southern tours, too. The musicians, being blacks, could not eat at most restaurants, nor sleep in most hotels, nor even use the rest rooms at ordinary gas stations. They traveled on old, bumpy buses, they slept in rooms rented in private homes in black neighborhoods. When they couldn't find a black restaurant, the manager or some other white would have to go into a store and order sandwiches for them all, which they would eat on the bus.

Once they had traveling with them the manager's wife, who was white. She was supposed to be responsible for the travel arrangements. She always tried to get a bus that had a soft seat in the back where Louis could lie down and sleep, for he had the weight of the show on his shoulders and needed as much rest as possible. On one visit to Memphis she discovered that the bus company had given them a bus with a hard wooden seat across the back. She protested. There was an argument. Somebody called the police, and when they saw a white woman on a bus filled with black men, they arrested the whole band, even though nobody had done anything wrong. There was nothing anybody could do about it. Finally the police said they would let the band go if they would put on a special broadcast from the Memphis radio station. Louis had no choice about it, but during the broadcast he dedicated one number to the Memphis police chief. The song was one of Louis's hits, "I'll Be Glad When You're Dead, You Rascal, You."

This constant work only increased Louis's lip problems. Sometimes the soreness was a little better, sometimes it was a little worse, but it never really went away. During this period the lip split again while he was playing a show at a theater in Philadelphia. Despite the fact that he was in almost constant pain, he insisted on playing the showy, high-note endings he believed people wanted.

Louis's personal life was troubled, too: His marriage to Lil was breaking up. Things had not always been smooth between them. They cared for each other, but they fought. The basic problem was that Lil was too ambitious for Louis. She wanted him to rise as far as his talents could take him, and as a consequence she was always urging him to do this or that. Frequently she simply took charge of things. She had told him how to dress and put him on a diet. She had urged him to leave Oliver, urged him to join Henderson in New York. Then she had insisted that he come back to Chicago to play under his own name at the Dreamland. However, she was the real boss of that band.

All of these things Lil did out of love for Louis, and she was right about most of them. Louis would not have accomplished as much as he had without Lil's prodding. Nonetheless, Louis had come to resent being constantly told what to do by his wife. Sometimes he would get angry and fight back, and over the years after he left Chicago for New York, the two began to drift apart.

Finally, in 1931 Lil realized that the marriage was never going to work as it should, and she suggested to Louis that they separate. Louis agreed. Lil Armstrong never remarried. She remained in love with Louis for the rest of her life. She continued to live in the house in Chicago she had bought for them, and she surrounded herself with mementos of their life together. They remained good friends, and whenever they happened to be in the same city, they would always get together and talk over old times.

Lil Armstrong was not a great jazz pianist, but she was well liked as a person by jazz people who knew her. She had been important to Louis because she'd given him the push he needed to start on his great career as a jazz musician and entertainer. In his heart Louis knew this, and he was always glad to see her when they got together in later life.

If the breakup with Lil were not enough, at just about the same time, in 1931, Louis decided to change managers. His new one was Johnny Collins, another tough, hard-drinking, fast-talking man with gangland connections. Why Louis decided to replace Rockwell with Collins we don't know. It was probably mainly a matter of Collins's talking Louis into it by promising him big money, movie deals, and so forth. So Louis signed with Collins.

It proved to be a bad mistake. For one thing, Louis was still under contract to Tommy Rockwell. Rockwell was no angel, but Collins was completely unscrupulous.

Troubles began almost immediately. Collins booked Louis and the band into a Chicago nightclub called The Showboat. The band went into the club in the afternoons to rehearse. Opening night was successful. On the second night of the engagement, as Louis was getting ready in his dressing room, there was a knock on the door. Louis always liked to have visitors in his dressing room and thought nothing of it. "Come in," he said.

The two people who entered, however, were not ordinary well-wishers come to collect Louis's autograph. A pair of tough-looking white men, they looked Louis up and down, and then told him: "You're opening in New York tomorrow night. Be there."

Louis stared back at them. "I have this engagement here in Chicago and I don't plan on traveling." Then he turned his back on them to show that he didn't want any further conversation on the matter. The moment he did so he heard a heavy steel click. He turned back and found himself facing a huge pistol. He looked at it for a moment, and then he said, "Well, I guess I will be opening in New York tomorrow."

The gangsters left, satisfied. Who they were Louis didn't know, but he suspected that they had been sent by Tommy Rockwell to scare Louis into living up to his contract with him. As soon as the gangsters were gone, Louis found Collins backstage and explained what had happened. Both of them were scared; these gangsters could be extremely dangerous. On the other hand, if Louis walked out on the Showboat engagement, the owners might also hire gangsters to threaten Louis. They were trapped.

They had to get Louis out of Chicago, Collins decided. But how? The gangsters were sure to be watching Louis to see if he was getting ready to go to New York.

So Collins called the band together and told them that there was trouble. If anybody asked them where Louis was, they were to say that they didn't know. He then told the band to start rehearsing. Louis went down the hall and hid in a phone booth, crouching down so that he would be below the glass. Shortly, the gangsters appeared at the rehearsal. When they didn't see Louis they assumed that he had gone to New York as they had ordered him. They left, and as soon as they were gone Louis slipped out of the club into a waiting cab, raced to the railroad station, and took the first train south. A couple of hours later Collins rounded up some more cabs, took the band to the station, and put them on a train to Louisville, Kentucky. When they arrived, they found Louis waiting there. Needless to say, they were overjoyed to see that he was safe.

Now Louis was in serious trouble. He could not go to New York for fear of Rockwell and his gangster friends, and he could not go to Chicago because he had skipped out on the Showboat engagement. America's two most important show business cities were closed to him. Johnny Collins's management was doing him little good.

The band played an engagement in Louisville and, playing one-nighters, worked its way south toward New Orleans, where Collins had booked the group into Suburban Gardens, an expensive restaurant just outside the city. It would be the first time that Louis had been back to his hometown since he had boarded the train ten years before with his cornet and that fish sandwich to go north to join King Oliver. So much had happened over those years that it seemed like a lifetime had passed. He had left New Orleans an obscure young cornetist whom nobody but a handful of black musicians and a few hustlers in black Storyville had ever heard of. He was coming back a burgeoning star, and the most widely respected jazz musician in the United States—and indeed the world, although he didn't realize that yet.

Nonetheless, he was unprepared for the reception that greeted him when he got off the train in New Orleans with his band. The street outside the station was thronged with people, both black and white. Strung overhead was a huge banner with his name on it. When he came into sight the mob roared and cheered. People from the crowd grabbed the band's suitcases and carried the whole band off for a banquet that had been prepared in Louis's honor. Louis was astounded; he had left his hometown unknown, and he had come back a hero.

Nor were audiences disappointed in him. The Suburban Gardens engagement had been scheduled for three weeks; so big were the crowds that the band stayed for three months. It was a moment of peace and quiet in the midst of troubles. Once it was over there was another grind of one-nighters. Finally, Collins decided to risk booking the band into a New York theater. They arrived, and before they could even open, Tommy Rockwell pounced with a court order saying that Louis was under contract to him and could not work without his permission. There was nothing to be done. The band fled for Chicago, where it made a few records. But Louis was in trouble in Chicago, too. All they could do was leave. The band broke up, and Louis went out to Los Angeles, where he played some jobs with a band hastily put together to back him.

It was all a mess. Collins, instead of doing anything to build Louis's career, had gotten him into trouble with the gangs and overworked him to the point where his lip was constantly sore and suffering damage that would be permanent. Jobs were booked haphazardly, records made on a catch-as-catch-can basis with inexperienced and inadequately rehearsed bands. And although Louis did not know it, Collins was stealing his money.

Making matters worse, the jazz fans who had worshipped him during the Hot Five days were beginning to talk critically. The great Louis Armstrong, they said, had "gone commercial." No longer was he playing those wonderful jazz solos like "West End Blues" and "Potato Head Blues" but was concentrating on putting out popular love songs.

Not everybody agreed with this judgment. Many of the musicians felt that Louis was playing as brilliantly as ever. What did it matter if he was playing popular tunes instead of the blues, or fronting a dance band instead of a hot jazz group? He still had that extraordinary sense of swing, that great ability to improvise. True, he was playing a sparer, perhaps more subtle style, but his playing was none the worse for that. So the argument went back and forth; but Louis was hurt that some of his old fans were turning away from him.

It was an old story, and a new one, too, because it

happens today, and it is worth taking a moment to look at it.

In the twentieth century, especially in the United States, but elsewhere in the world, too, entertainment has become one of the major industries. Think of all the records that are made each year, all the television shows put on, the hundreds of radio stations dotted across the United States, tens of thousands of video games, the endless stream of movies coming into theaters, and professional sports leagues that grow year by year to the point where it is hard even for sports fans to keep track of all the dozens of hockey, football, basketball, baseball, and soccer teams.

This huge industry takes in billions of dollars a year. Fortunes can be made. Stars of whatever kind can, and do, make grotesquely high incomes, sometimes running into tens of millions of dollars. But the real money is made by people behind the scenes—managers, record producers, and the large corporations that own movie companies, sports complexes, television stations.

This enormous entertainment industry had begun to take shape in the 1890s, and by 1929, when Tommy Rockwell was beginning to promote Louis Armstrong, it had become clear that there were huge amounts of money in it. Inevitably, it attracted greedy men who were interested only in money and had no concern with making good music, fine movies, worthwhile radio shows. Frequently using tactics that were unethical, and often illegal, these men fought each other for places at the top of the corporations that controlled the various segments of show business—the theater chains, the record companies, the movie studios. These segments of show business often interlocked; a movie company might own the theaters in which its films were shown, a record company might own a company that managed the singers and bandleaders it had under contract.

To these men who controlled various aspects of show business, the secret of it all was to get control of what everybody called "talent." By the word "talent," they meant the performers who were at the heart of the entertainment business, who were what the business was really all about.

Few of the businessmen who ran American entertainment knew how to act, how to play a musical instrument, what ingredients went into a play to make it successful. Those secrets were reserved for the "talent." But the smartest of them had a sense of what would work with the public and what wouldn't. They could spot a young singer or dancer in a smoky backstreet nightclub and recognize that he or she had that special something that would get across to audiences. They weren't always right, of course, but they were right often enough. They would sign up young performers, often to long-term contracts, arrange publicity campaigns for them, get them into good theaters and clubs through their contacts, build them up, and scoop substantial amounts of money off the top. Tommy Rockwell was such a man. He couldn't carry a tune, could hardly remember the names of songs, but he had an intuition for talent and made a lot of money as record producer, talent booker and manager, and music publisher. To put it bluntly, men like Rockwell fed off talent. Granted, many performers have poor heads for business, and most of them need expert guidance in building their careers. Nonetheless, too often their managers and others involved with them are primarily out to make themselves rich, and they do it at the expense of the performers.

In addition, the American entertainment industry has always been tainted with criminal influence. Gangsters did—and sometimes still do—own clubs. Through this opening they sometimes got in on record contracts, movie deals, music publishing businesses. Gangsters have been known to murder performers who didn't obey orders.

During the years when Louis Armstrong was rising to fame, black performers were especially victimized by the entertainment industry. In the first place, many of them, like Louis, had been brought up to believe that they had to do what whites told them to do. Louis, remember, had grown up in a city where he could not even walk in certain places without the approval of whites. Being brought up that way, he and many other blacks found it very difficult to stand up to the whites, like Tommy Rockwell and Johnny Collins, who ran things.

Second, although blacks could be successful as performers, it was almost impossible for them to work their way up to become important executives at record companies, theater chains, radio stations. The good jobs were reserved for whites.

For the black performers this meant that they were at the mercy of whites. And too frequently the whites who controlled show business believed that blacks were there to be cheated. They felt that blacks should be grateful to have show business careers at all and shouldn't complain if they didn't get the money they were owed.

Louis Armstrong, as he rose into stardom, was drawn into this complex, corrupt, and, to some extent, criminal entertainment industry. He was not well educated, and he had never had much experience in business. Nonetheless, he was intelligent, and he had seen a good deal of life in the slums of New Orleans. He knew about human beings, the bad as well as the good, and although he didn't understand how show business worked in detail, he had a pretty fair idea of what was going on around him. And he knew, when he thought about it, that he was almost certainly being cheated by his manager, the record companies, the theater owners. One other thing he knew was that he couldn't do anything about it. He would have to accept it and try to forget about it.

Tommy Rockwell, at least, had done constructive things for Louis, getting him that first big break in *Hot Chocolates* and seeing to it that he got the best songs to record. Johnny Collins never did anything for

Louis except to keep him working, often in the worst circumstances, and take his money. And by the end of 1931, Armstrong was suffering in all aspects of his life—physical, financial, artistic. His lip was battered, his bands were hastily put together and hastily broken up, his finances were in disarray, gangsters appeared whenever he went to New York or Chicago. His spirits were sagging. What had started out so well in 1929 was all smashed. Where would he turn? He drifted through to the spring of 1932; and then suddenly he decided to get as far away from it all as he could. He would go to Europe.

# CHAPTER TWELVE

Whose idea it was for Louis to go to Europe we don't know, but it was a natural one. The simple truth is that things were better in Europe for blacks. They were hardly perfect; blacks could not get into all hotels, all restaurants, or live in all areas of European cities like London and Paris. Armstrong himself was turned down by a dozen hotels on his first trip to London. Nonetheless, blacks could get into some good hotels, some good restaurants in Europe. In the United States they could hardly get into any except those especially meant for them in their own areas.

Just as there had been a boom in black entertainment in the United States during the 1920s, so there was a similar one in Europe. Black musicians, singers, and dancers toured Europe and came back with stories about how much better things were for blacks there.

Louis, of course, had heard these stories. Moreover, he had heard vaguely that English record collectors, especially musicians, were eagerly buying his records. The English—and Europeans in general—were interested in American popular music, but it was mainly ordinary dance music that they were listening to. However, by the end of the 1920s a few jazz records had reached England. English musicians and a tiny handful of jazz fans were beginning to learn about the music. Then, in the fall of 1929, some editors from the English musicians' paper, *Melody Maker*, came to New York. They heard Armstrong at Connie's Inn, Duke Ellington at the Cotton Club, and other American jazz musicians. They were astonished by jazz, and they wrote about it in the *Melody Maker* when they returned. At about the same time an English record company called Parlophone began to bring out a few of the best American jazz records each month, including Louis's best records from the Hot Five series. English musicians were astounded by his playing, and very quickly Louis developed an English following. The general public didn't yet know much about it, but musicians and jazz fans were very enthusiastic about his music.

Louis had been told that he had fans in England although he had no idea how avid they were. But going abroad would get him away from his troubles, and he was glad to go. Unfortunately Collins, in his typical fashion, made few arrangements. He booked Louis for two weeks at London's famous Palladium, but that was all he did. He failed to arrange for hotel rooms, or a band to back Louis.

When the English musicians realized that Louis was actually coming they were ecstatic. The *Melody Maker* gave the news a front-page headline. The promoters hastily put together a band made up mainly of black Americans living in Paris, and the British waited in breathless anticipation for the great jazz musician.

They were not disappointed. The engagement at the Palladium was a great success. A few musicians complained about Louis's showy high-note endings and his clowning around on the stage, but most were entranced, and many of them came every day during the whole two-week stay. It was during this English trip that Louis acquired his famous nickname "Satchmo," a shortened form of the earlier nickname "Satchelmouth."

Louis was excited by the reception he received. It was startling to him that these people so far from the roots of jazz in New Orleans had come to love the music, and especially his own playing. He could have made an extended tour around England, but unfortunately Johnny Collins had failed to arrange anything. Louis played a few casual jobs, made a visit to Paris, and then, in November, headed home. On the last night at sea the musicians in the ship's orchestra gave Louis a dinner party. On the first night back in New York he went up to Connie's Inn, where he was given a tremendous ovation by the crowd. There was no doubt of it now: Whatever turmoil his career was in, he was a star.

Despite the fact that the English tour had been badly managed by Collins, it had been good for Louis. It had allowed him to take it easy for a while and to rest his lip. He came back in good spirits, already planning another trip to England.

But once again Collins set about working Louis as hard as he could. There were theater dates and dance jobs, with unplanned and haphazard recording sessions slipped in wherever they could fit. Louis's lip got worse and worse. By January 1933, his lip was painfully sore. It improved a little by the spring, but by April it was in such bad shape that one of the other trumpet players in the band was playing the opening choruses of tunes that Louis usually took, and other members of the band were being given many solos so Louis would only have to play the solos at the end, with their showy high-register climaxes.

Collins and the people from the record company should have insisted that Louis take a vacation and rest his lip. However, they saw Louis as just another black entertainer to be worked as hard as possible, and they kept pushing him to play the next job, to cut the required six records at each record session, regardless of what was happening to his lip. Louis, of course, should have protested, but once again he found it difficult to stand up to the white bosses. Louis didn't like making a fuss or causing trouble, so he allowed these callous men to drive him like a mule.

Furthermore, the men in the band were becoming increasingly unhappy. Collins was constantly trying to cheat them out of their salaries, which were not very high to begin with, and put the money in his own pocket. They protested, and, finally, they said they wouldn't play anymore unless Collins paid them what he owed them. Collins was forced to give in for the moment, but he was angry at them, and as soon as they had completed the engagements they were contracted for, he fired the whole band and set about planning another European tour.

This time he made better arrangements. There was to be a stay at the Holborn Empire, a London theater, and then a tour of the British Isles. So they sailed, and Louis began the Holborn theater job. He had not been playing it too long when he finally woke up to the fact that Collins had been stealing from him. Collins always collected the money for the jobs and turned over a certain amount to Louis. Out of the rest he was supposed to be sending some money to Lil as alimony, and sending some to the United States government for Louis's taxes. Instead, he had been putting the money in his own pocket.

Suddenly Louis was informed that he owed both Lil and the government a great deal of money. This was more than even the mild-mannered Louis could take. He blew up at Collins, shouting and cursing, and fired him on the spot. Collins tried to explain, but there was no explanation, and Louis turned his back on him. So Collins left for the United States; out of spite, he took Louis's passport with him.

Louis was able to get another passport, but he was now faced with a mountain of debts. He was not eager to go back to the United States; Europe seemed more friendly to him, and so he stayed on through all of the next year. But in the fall of 1934 his lip collapsed again. He was forced to cancel a tour halfway through. The promoters were angry and threatened to sue him. Louis could no longer work in Europe, at least for the time being. So in January 1935, he came back to the United States.

His career was almost wrecked. He had not recorded in the United States for almost two years, he owed a lot of money, he still had not straightened out his contractual problems with Tommy Rockwell, he was worried about gangsters. All he had to show for six years of hard work since his breakthrough in *Hot Chocolates* were some three dozen 78 rpm records—about three and a half hours of music. He had no way of knowing that fifty years later many of these records would be considered jazz classics. All he knew was that his lip was ruined, he was deeply in debt, and he was, if not forgotten, out of work.

Then he met a man named Joe Glaser, a white. Glaser was a fascinating character. He was born into a solid middle-class family in Chicago. His father was a doctor, and everybody expected that Joe would grow up to be a doctor, too. Instead, as he got into his teens, he began hanging around the black and tan cabarets of the South Side, just at the time that Louis was playing in those clubs. Glaser struck up acquaintanceships with the gangsters who owned many of these clubs and hung around them. In a short time he was "fronting" for them—that is to say, he would put his name to various deals that were actually being made by the mobsters.

Hanging around the black and tans, Glaser also got to know a lot of the hustlers, their women, and the musicians who worked there. During these years of the late 1920s he and Louis got to know each other. They were not exactly great friends, but they were friendly enough. Joe Glaser seemed to Louis to be another one of those hard-cursing, hard-drinking tough men whom he so greatly admired—another man like Benny Williams, Tommy Rockwell, and Johnny Collins. Fortunately for Louis, Joe Glaser had another side to him.

When Louis arrived back in the United States in January of 1935, Joe Glaser was in difficulties himself. He had ridden high during the 1920s, but when the Chicago gangsters had had their wings clipped by the reform government, he'd gone down with them. Then, in the early 1930s, he got into serious trouble with the police. Nobody knows exactly what happened, but it may have concerned a murder. Glaser's gangland friends still had enough power to keep him from going to jail, but he had to leave Chicago for a while. In 1935, Joe Glaser badly needed a lift.

Louis knew that, and he also respected Glaser. He recognized that underneath Glaser's tough front, there was something else. Joe Glaser was a man of his word. If he made a promise, he would keep it. Moreover, Glaser was basically kind and generous. He would shout and curse, but in the next breath he would offer to lend you money or help you out in some other way. Louis knew all of this, and he asked Glaser to take charge of his career. For Glaser it was an important break. Louis's career was in bad shape, but he was still admired by the jazz fans and was popular with the general public. Glaser could still make money with Louis; and so he set about doing it. He made an arrangement to pay off Tommy Rockwell. He used his own gangland connections to smooth things out with the mobsters. He made a deal with both Lil and the U.S. government to pay them off a little at a time. He signed Louis to a contract with Decca, a new record company that was just starting up. He arranged to have the Luis Russell band back Louis, and he put Louis to work.

The partnership between Louis Armstrong and Joe Glaser was a curious one. Paradoxically, it was the man from the tough slum who was the self-effacing, sensitive artist, the man from the nice middle-class family who was the hard-cursing tough. And there is no doubt that at first Joe Glaser was doing what Johnny Collins had done—scooping off far too large a share of Louis's earnings. But quickly there grew up between the two men a feeling of respect and affection. Glaser was riding up out of his difficulties on Louis's back. And although he may have helped himself to too much of the money, he always had Louis's best interests in mind. He wanted Louis to be happy, rich, and famous, and he did everything he could to achieve these goals. Using Louis as his first stepping-stone, he became rich and powerful in the American entertainment business. And through shrewd management he made Louis into one of the most famous entertainers of his time.

# CHAPTER THIRTEEN

Despite Louis's long absence from the United States and the lack of new records to remind the public about him, he had not been forgotten. And between 1935 and 1940, under Joe Glaser's skillful management, Louis Armstrong rose to a height of popularity reached by no other black man or woman before that time. By the end of 1935 he was being written up in major magazines like *Esquire* and *Vanity Fair*. In 1936 he appeared in the first of a long series of movies, *Pennies from Heaven*, with Bing Crosby. He had been in short films before, but from this point on he would make at least one film a year, usually playing alongside major stars.

In 1937 he began broadcasting on sponsored radio shows. This was a very important breakthrough. There was no television then, and radio was an important medium. At the time the soap, breakfast food, appliance, and other companies who sponsored radio programs hesitated to use black performers, for fear that whites, especially southern whites, would object and stop buying their products. But Louis had such wide acceptance that sponsors were willing to hire him for their shows. In fact, Louis even had his own sponsored radio show for a brief period, the first black to have one.

During these years, a new paper devoted to popular music, called *Down Beat*, began to run popularity polls of band leaders and musicians. Louis was always at the top of these polls, or near it, as the country's favorite trumpet player. In 1940, he was back on Broadway in a modern musical version of Shakespeare's famous *A Midsummer Night's Dream*, which was called *Swinging the Dream*. The show was not very good, but Louis got excellent reviews for his work in it.

Between 1935 and 1940, with Joe Glaser's good management, Louis Armstrong became one of America's top show-business stars. He was not at the pinnacle—that place was reserved for the most famous movie stars. But everywhere in America people knew him and enjoyed his music.

Of course the person mainly responsible for Louis's success was not Joe Glaser, but Louis himself. Even when he was singing the silliest tune, there was a warmth and naturalness that came through to audiences. He seemed such a friendly person that it was impossible not to like him. And he was a consummate musician. It didn't matter that his voice was rough; he always sang in tune, with that infectious swing, so that he made even poor tunes sound as if they were wonderful.

All of this success, however, was not without its cost. Neither Joe Glaser nor Decca, Louis's record company, was very much interested in great jazz, or great music of any kind, for that matter. They just wanted to make money, and they encouraged Louis to stick with the most popular kind of music. Some of it wasn't at all bad, but a lot of it was way below the artistry of the Hot Fives. Not that there's anything wrong with a good popular song well played; popular music can be wonderful. But Louis Armstrong had been, ten years earlier, the greatest jazz musician alive, pouring out one beautiful, deeply felt chorus after another. He was no longer doing that. Much of what he played was just routine popular music. Some of it consisted of silly novelty songs. Worse, a good deal of his repertoire was made up of songs that depicted blacks as lazy, happy-go-lucky folk who loved to pick cotton and were not very intelligent.

Of course, Louis Armstrong could hardly help bringing beauty to anything he played. He always swung, even when he was playing a simple melody very straight. At times, too, he played some wonderful jazz, for example, on his versions of "Struttin' with Some Barbecue" and "I Double Dare You," in 1936. But far too often he was content to play his solo on a tune the same way night after night.

The truth is that by this time Louis himself was far more interested in being popular and making money than he was in playing good jazz. Of course, Joe Glaser and the people at Decca wanted him to make commercial music. But he could have insisted on mixing in some good jazz, as other musicians such as Benny

Goodman and Duke Ellington were doing. He did not, however, and he did not because the main thing for him was hearing that applause. No matter how famous he got, he was never sure that people really liked him, and he had to go on night after night proving to himself that he was loved.

By 1940, then, Louis had become a star. But anybody who looked closely would have seen that not everything was quite as rosy as it appeared on the surface. A new generation of music fans was coming along, and they had new heroes, like Glenn Miller and Tommy Dorsey. These band leaders were not in Louis's class as jazz musicians, but their bands played slick, clean dance tunes in the new "swing" style that grew up after 1935. By 1940 Louis was beginning to drop in the polls. The critics were writing that he had gone commercial, and they didn't take him seriously as a jazz musician anymore.

Even the musicians who had been in awe of Louis were turning away from him. The older ones, who had been learning from him for years, continued to admire him, but the younger musicians coming along were learning from other trumpet players, such as Roy Eldridge. Louis was becoming outdated.

For a time the problems were not apparent. The United States had been drawn into World War II in 1941. Many musicians were drafted into the army. There was a shortage of bands, and Louis was able to work as much as ever. But when the war ended, suddenly the demand for bands dropped. By 1946 Louis's stock had hit bottom. While in the 1930s he had been making twenty records a year, in 1946 he cut exactly one. Where he had always been at or near the top of the dance band polls in *Down Beat* and other music magazines, in 1946 he didn't make the list. The musicians admired him for the way he'd played in the past and what he could still do when he tried, and the critics respected him for his role in the creation of jazz, but young music fans had no interest in him at all. Although he still was working regularly, it was clear that there was trouble ahead.

But if his professional life was in trouble, his private life was improving. In 1938 Louis happened to be playing the Cotton Club in Harlem. He noticed a very pretty girl in the chorus line. Her name, he discovered, was Lucille Wilson, and she had been dancing at the Cotton Club for several years.

Lucille was not only pretty, she was smart and sophisticated. She had grown up in New York and, through her experience at the Cotton Club, knew her way around show business. Louis very quickly became eager to know her better. Whenever he had the chance he would get into a conversation with her, but that was not always easy, because he was on stage playing and singing most of the time. To show her that he was interested in her he would have dinners sent up to her dressing room during her breaks.

Louis was of course a big star, and Lucille was just an obscure dancer at the club. She was very flattered, but worried: What did this big star want with her?

She decided it would be best not to get involved. Besides, he was on the road and away from New York most of the time.

Louis and his orchestra had to play half an hour for dancing after each one of the Cotton Club's shows. During this time Lucille would go to her dressing room, quickly get dressed, and slip out of the club. Louis was puzzled. Why was she avoiding him? One night, after the show was finished, he told one of the other trumpeters to play his part during the dance set. He jumped off the stage and managed to catch up to Lucille just as she was leaving the club. "I don't know where you're going," he told her, "and I don't know who you're going with. But man, woman, or child, I'm coming, too."

Lucille was startled, but he was so determined she could not refuse him.

As they walked away from the club, Louis said, "Why are you avoiding me?"

"I don't think it's a good idea to get involved with a big star like you. Besides, you're away so much of the time."

"Well, you're not going to get away from me anymore," Louis said. He was true to his word. He continued to see her during their breaks, and when he was out of town he phoned her frequently. It took two years of persuasion before Lucille agreed to marry him. But on October 12, 1942, they were married. It turned out to be a long and happy marriage. Lucille didn't interfere with Louis's music or business affairs, but she traveled with him frequently and helped to see that things went smoothly around him so he could concentrate on his playing. She also bought a house for them in Corona, a section of the borough of Queens in New York City. At first Louis said he didn't want a house; he was content to live in hotels. But once Lucille had fixed up the house, he decided he liked it; and when he was off the road he was happy to spend his time there, resting, watching baseball games on television, or playing his large collection of records.

But Louis's happy marriage didn't solve the problems of his fading career. That needed something else; but what was the answer?

Joe Glaser gave the whole matter some thought. By 1946 Glaser had become a great success in the music business. He had a lot of clients working for him besides Louis, and he didn't really need him anymore. But Glaser was loyal to Louis and determined to help him rise once again.

Glaser was aware of two trends in the music business. One was the growing popularity of singers. There had always been singers, of course, but mostly they worked with the big name bands. Frank Sinatra sang with Tommy Dorsey; Ella Fitzgerald sang with Chick Webb; Peggy Lee sang with Benny Goodman. The main star was the leader, not the singer.

But during the 1940s listeners became more and more interested in the singers. Singers became, in fact, just as important as the leaders. By 1946 many singers had left the bands and gone off on their own, using just a small group to accompany them. Louis Armstrong was a singer. Joe Glaser wondered if there were something to be done with that.

The second trend was, surprisingly, the revival of the old New Orleans style of jazz that Louis had done so much to popularize twenty years earlier. Even though it had lost out to the big bands, there had always been people who preferred it—who thought it was a stronger and more emotional music than the dance music of the swing bands. Here and there a few players had managed to keep the old music alive. And in the years around 1940 several jazz critics were writing books trying to persuade people to go back to the old New Orleans style.

Many of them did. Among them were a lot of high school students. These young people began hunting around in secondhand stores for old, used jazz records, especially ones by Jelly Roll Morton, King Oliver, and of course the famous Hot Fives of Louis Armstrong. Sometimes they could buy these records for as little as five cents. The records had not been available in the stores for ten years. Now young people began listening to them and swapping them with their friends as well.

Soon the record companies realized that there was still an audience—small, but growing—for the old New Orleans music. They began reissuing records by the Oliver Creole Jazz Band, and Louis Armstrong and his Hot Five. Musicians who had always loved the old music better than the music of the dance bands began to form groups to play it, and by 1946 there was a substantial interest in New Orleans music, or Dixieland, as it was now called. Dixieland was certainly not as popular as the singers, for instance Frank Sinatra, who had huge audiences of teenagers following them around. But it was popular enough, and so Joe Glaser decided to try Armstrong with a Dixieland band, once again playing the music he had learned as a boy in black Storyville.

The popularity of Dixieland caught the attention of some people in Hollywood, too. They decided to make a movie about the days when jazz was burgeoning in New Orleans. Very quickly they chose Louis Armstrong to have a part in it. The movie was to be called *New Orleans*, and in the summer of 1946 they started making it. In the movie Louis took the part of a New Orleans musician, playing with a Dixieland band that included Kid Ory and Louis's old friend, Zutty Singleton, one of the rare times that he played with either of these men after the Hot Five days.

The movie, everyone was sure, would help to promote the revival of Dixieland. A concert at Carnegie Hall was then arranged, featuring Louis playing with both his big band and a small Dixieland band. The concert was a success and got a lot of reviews in the newspapers. Encouraged, Louis agreed to play another concert consisting entirely of Dixieland jazz at Town Hall in New York on May 17, 1947. Playing with Armstrong would be some of the greatest names in jazz, among them Jack Teagarden on trombone, Bobby

Hackett on second cornet, Big Sid Catlett on drums, and Bob Haggart on bass. This was the concert the jazz fans had been waiting for. For years they had been hoping that Louis would someday again play with a real jazz band. Now he was going to do it.

On the night of May 17, Town Hall was packed, and when Louis was introduced the audience burst into tumultuous cheers and applause. Louis began the concert by playing some of the tunes he had made with the Hot Five and continued with other tunes on which he had played some of his most famous solos. He played beautifully, and the other men, inspired by the return of Louis to jazz, were at the top of their form. The concert was an enormous success, got wonderful reviews in the papers, and is remembered today as one of the great evenings in jazz—the evening when Louis came home to his music.

A few weeks later the movie *New Orleans* opened. Louis and much the same band that had appeared at the Town Hall concert played a concert for the movie's premiere. It was broadcast around the United States and was also a great success. It was now abundantly clear that Louis's star was once again rising, and that his future lay in playing and singing with a Dixieland band. At the end of the summer Joe Glaser organized a small jazz band to back Louis, which included trombonist Jack Teagarden and a pal of Louis's from the Chicago days, pianist Earl Hines. In August, the band opened at a Hollywood jazz club called Billy Berg's. A lot of celebrities from the music business came for the opening. The press was full of stories; even *Time* gave the band a big write-up. Suddenly, Louis Armstrong was everywhere in the papers. From that moment on, Joe Glaser was able to book the new group, which was called Louis Armstrong and His All Stars, for top prices everywhere.

After 1947 Louis Armstrong's star continued to rise with hardly a dip. In 1949 he was chosen to be King of the Zulus at the famous Mardi Gras parade in his hometown of New Orleans. The King of the Zulus was usually an ordinary person from the city, but New Orleanians were so proud of Louis that they chose him. Not only was the story played up in all the newspapers around the country, but it put Louis on the cover of *Time* magazine. The same year Louis had his first big hit, "Blueberry Hill," which rose high on the charts. In 1952 the readers of *Down Beat*, the jazz and popular music magazine, elected him "the most important musical figure of all time." In 1954 he published a memoir of his boyhood in New Orleans called *Satchmo: My Life in New Orleans*. In 1956 he had another big hit with "The Theme from the Threepenny Opera," better known as "Mack the Knife." In 1957 a famous television anchor named Edward R. Murrow made an hour-long show about Louis, which was later made into a movie. At the same time Decca put out an elaborate four-volume *Musical Autobiography* of Louis, made up mainly of remakes of his most famous tunes from the past. He was appearing in a new movie almost every year, he was constantly a guest on top television shows, he recorded frequently, and he was as busy as he could possibly be playing nightclubs, restaurants, and theaters.

He toured abroad, too. Fans everywhere thronged to hear him. He toured Europe, Africa, Asia. He made a series of goodwill tours for the State Department. From this he got the nickname "Ambassador Satch." Finally, in 1963 he had a smash hit with the tune "Hello, Dolly." The record made the *Billboard* chart in February, entering as number 76. It rose steadily week by week into May, when it pushed the Beatles' "Can't Buy Me Love" out of the number one spot. Louis Armstrong, the boy from the New Orleans slum, was at the top of the world of popular music.

# CHAPTER FOURTEEN

When Louis Armstrong died on July 6, 1971, he was one of the most famous entertainers in the world. President Richard Nixon issued a special message of sorrow from the White House, and his funeral was attended by dignitaries and show business celebrities, including the mayor of New York City, the governor of New York State, and fellow musicians like Frank Sinatra and Bing Crosby. Down in New Orleans fifteen thousand people gathered to hear many jazz bands play at a memorial service for him.

Today his records are as popular as ever. Go into a record store anyplace in the world, and there will be a rack full of Louis Armstrong records, ranging from the earliest of the Hot Fives to his greatest popular hit, "Hello, Dolly," made when he was sixty-five years old. Several books have been written about him, and in music archives jazz researchers dig out the tiny details of his life and his music. In New Orleans there is a Louis Armstrong Park; in New York there is a Louis Armstrong Stadium.

The story of Louis Armstrong's life tells us several things. One of them is how hard it was for a black of Louis Armstrong's generation to exploit his talent to the fullest. Louis was handicapped in almost every way. He was shy, uneducated, lacked decent musical training, was brutally poor as a child, and had no support from his father. How could he possibly be expected to challenge a social system that was determined to keep blacks in their place and exploit them in any way it could? He had learned as a boy to do what he was told, and even as a grown man and a big star, he found it hard to go against the wishes of the whites around him. Too often, instead of thinking through what he might do with his music, he listened to other people.

A second lesson to be learned from Louis's story is how difficult it is for a person of great talent to keep his or her artistic integrity. Louis Armstrong spent most of his working career playing in commercial dance and show bands, whose function was solely to entertain. The great jazz that he played, and the great records he left us, were incidental. The Hot Fives were not supposed to be great art, but commercial records to be sold quickly and forgotten. It was Louis's inescapable genius that made them into treasures. The same is true of many of the recordings he made during the big band days, and later with his Dixieland All Stars. The great music on them was an accident; nobody planned them to be anything other than quick-selling records, but once again Louis's genius simply burst through. During his career he was always surrounded by people telling him to be funny, make faces, grin, play high notes, get that applause, and forget about anything else. Nobody cared that Louis might have something personal to *say* through his music, and rarely did any of those in charge of his career encourage him to even think about it. Make money—that was the whole point.

Is it any different today? Are talented young people interested in expressing new and personal ideas about the world and themselves, or do they believe that the most important thing is to become a star? Do they believe that it is better to try to discover the truth about things—as hard as that often is—or is the most important thing to make money?

Given the pressures on talent, we can only be grateful that Louis Armstrong left us as much magnificent music as he did. There are moments of beauty in everything he did. Even in his most commercial work there are notes that sparkle, motions that touch. And in his best work he left us a monument—not as large as we would like, but many, many hours of brilliant music for us to enjoy. And no doubt people will be enjoying it for a long time to come.

## If you want to know more about Louis Armstrong. . .

**F**or readers who would like to know more about Louis Armstrong, there are a number of books available. First, there is Louis's own book, *Satchmo: My Life in New Orleans*. It is not entirely accurate, but it gives a good picture of Louis's youth as he remembered it. For a more scholarly look at his life there is my own book, *Louis Armstrong: An American Genius*, which discusses his life and analyzes many of his records in detail. There is also a book called *Louis* by two Englishmen, Max Jones and John Chilton, which is especially good on Louis's European trips. And there is a small book containing a long interview with Louis by Richard Meryman called *Louis Armstrong*. Most of these books can be found in libraries.

Readers interested in the details of Armstrong's recordings will find them most accurately arranged in Hans Westerberg's *Boy from New Orleans: Louis "Satchmo" Armstrong*. However, this book will be hard to find. More easily available are standard jazz discographies, which most music libraries have.

More important than the books, however, is the music Louis left us. Most of the records he made before the All Star period beginning in 1947 are available in one form or another. French CBS has issued a set, called *V.S.O.P.*, of all the OKeh recordings, including the Hot Fives and the early big-band records. Record stores specializing in jazz are likely to have this set. Columbia has issued in the United States a four-record set called *The Louis Armstrong Story*, which contains a good selection of these OKehs. They are available in most record stores and libraries that have jazz records.

Armstrong's big-band records for Victor are complete on a two-record set call *Young Louis Armstrong 1932–1933*. Most of the Decca big-band songs from 1935 to 1946 are on *Louis Armstrong and His Orchestra* on the Australian Swaggie label, which record stores with good stocks of jazz are likely to have. These same Deccas are also available in rather mixed form on MCA's Jazz Heritage series, which most record stores have.

Any record store will have a great number of records from Armstrong's All Star period, but because there are so many from this time it is difficult to know what you will turn up. Among the best are the four-album set called *Satchmo: A Musical Biography of Louis Armstrong*; *Satch Plays Fats*; *Louis Armstrong's Greatest Hits*; *Ella and Louis*; and *Louis Armstrong Plays W. C. Handy*. Most of these should be relatively easy to find.

However, it will be much harder to find some of his earliest recordings. There is a Fantasy album called *Louis Armstrong and King Oliver* that contains a good sample of the Olivers and most of the Red Onion Jazz

Babies. The Smithsonian Collection has a good double album called *Louis Armstrong and Sidney Bechet in New York*, which contains some blues accompaniments, some Fletcher Henderson recordings, some Clarence Williams Blue Fives, and others. Armstrong's accompaniments for Bessie Smith are on Columbia's *The Bessie Smith Story, Volume 1*. Many of Louis's important solos with Fletcher Henderson are in a boxed set called *The Fletcher Henderson Story: A Study in Frustration*, but this set will be hard to locate.

# INDEX